LONDON'S WEST END CINEMAS

LONDON'S WEST END CINEMAS

by Allen Eyles & Keith Skone

Keytone Publications

Copyright © 1984 and 1991 by Allen
Eyles and Keith Skone

ISBN 0 9514313 1 5 (hardback)
     0 9514313 2 3 (paperback)

Publishers: Keith Skone, Tony Moss,
John Fernee
Text and production: Allen Eyles
Research: Allen Eyles, Keith Skone
Sales manager: Keith Skone

Published 1991 by
Keytone Publications
40 Vicarage Road
Sutton
Surrey SM1 1QN
Telephone: (081) 644 2650

Acknowledgements

We are most grateful to those organisa-
tions and individuals who have helped us
with illustrations – sources are acknow-
ledged in the captions where known.
Other illustrations are usually from the
collections of the authors. Thanks are
due to Don Graham, Brian Gauntlet,
Tony Bloom, Chris Green and Malcolm
Webb who made it possible for interior
photographs to be taken. Two books by
Raymond Mander and Joe Mitchenson –
Theatres of London and *Lost Theatres of
London* (both New English Library,
1975 and 1976) were very helpful in
establishing the history of West End live
theatres featured in this book. David
Trevor-Jones was of great assistance
where photographs in the CTA Archive
were concerned. John House and the
late John Squires provided valuable
additional data for this second edition.
And we remain particularly indebted to
Shirley Hind.

□ **Facing title page: REGAL (later ODEON)
MARBLE ARCH** *(from BFI Stills, Posters
and Designs collection)*. **On title page:
detail of staircase from EROS Piccadilly
Circus, now preserved in the Museum of
London** *(ph: John Edwards for the Museum
of London)*.

Typeset and printed by
Lithosphere Printing Co-operative
82/90 Queensland Road
London N7 7AW

Contents

Introduction 6

Maps 9

London's West End
Cinemas in chronological
order 13

Some Club Cinemas 117

Video Cinema 117

Theatres as Cinemas 118

Name Index 120

Introduction

This survey covers all the buildings that were designed and erected as public cinemas in London's West End, and other buildings that functioned as public cinemas for a substantial period of time.

The first proper cinemas were not established until films had proved that they were a lasting attraction rather than a temporary novelty. In fact, the first paying audience in Britain went to the pictures on 20 February 1986. The occasion was the showing of a programme of short films made by Louis and Auguste Lumière in France with their Cinématographe. This same programme had been premiered in Paris on 28 December 1895 and an entrepreneur friend of the Lumières called Félicien Trewey (a former music hall performer) brought it over to the Polytechnic's Marlborough Hall in Regent Street. The show attracted such attention that even *The Times* reviewed it and crowds flocked there, although it was primarily aimed to gain the attention of people of influence and especially theatrical impresarios who were offered the Cinématographe and trained staff to operate it for £100 per week. The terms were accepted by the Empire music hall in Leicester Square which opened the same programme on 9 March and retained the Cinématographe for eighteen months as a twenty-minute star attraction on the bill.

A rival film show, Robert W. Paul's Theatrograph (later Animatograph), which had made its commercial debut at Olympia, took up residence at the Egyptian Hall in Piccadilly from 19 March and at the Alhambra music hall in Leicester Square for a lengthy run from 25 March.

The first specialised cinemas in America offered the novelty of *Hale's Tours of the World*. These were travel films, usually shot abroad, that ran for about ten minutes and were shown in small auditoria made up to resemble railway carriages: the lights went down, a blind was raised at the front end of the carriage and films were rear-projected onto the screen while a live narrator described what was being shown, and the floor vibrated to suggest a train in motion, giving the patron the impression of seeing the views out of the front of a moving train. For London, Henry Iles bought a franchise from the American inventor, George C. Hale, and opened up at 165 Oxford Street in 1906, with the daringly democratic idea of charging sixpence admission for all seats.

The most active cinema entrepreneur in the early days of West End cinemagoing was Montagu A. Pyke, whose circuit opened three well-appointed cinemas in the West End – at Oxford Street, Windmill Street and Cambridge Circus, along with many others in the London suburbs.

The West End Cinema Theatre (later the Rialto) was in a class of its own in the pre-war period, designed and built to legitimate theatre standards, although, at Marble Arch, Israel Davis provided a Pavilion fit for a King and Queen (to visit occasionally).

The new Tivoli in the Strand became the West End's largest cinema when it opened in 1923 with over 2,000 seats. The big American film-making companies were becoming interested in having West End outlets to control the launch of their films in this country – Paramount (as Famous Players) leased the London Pavilion for a while from 1923 and Metro-Goldwyn-Mayer leased the Tivoli in 1925. In 1926, Paramount built and opened the Plaza as its own outlet, subsequently adding the Carlton. Metro-Goldwyn-Mayer moved from the Tivoli to its specially-built Empire in Leicester Square in 1928, a spectacular cinema seating over 3,000, the largest ever built in central London.

Marble Arch was now somewhat out on a limb – making life as difficult for the huge Regal, opened in 1928, as it has for the replacement Odeon of today.

□□□□

After the Regal, no new cinemas were built in the West End proper for more than five years. There was, however, the opening up of the Victoria area as a major cinemagoing centre with the construction of two large picture palaces. These were the Metropole, and the remarkable New Victoria which introduced some dazzlingly innovative ideas in cinema design to this country.

Several new live theatres were built and opened from 1928 to 1931, but most took the precaution of incorporating a projection box to provide for alternative use, and many of them were soon forced to play films. In the case of the Piccadilly, the big screen proved a temporary diversion but the Dominion quickly settled down to a long career as a cinema. Other new theatres like the Prince Edward, Cambridge and Phoenix were principally used for evening trade shows by the film distributors. In addition, as part of the general decline of music hall in favour of cinema, the London Pavilion and Alhambra went over to movies. Projection facilities were installed at most existing theatres and put to occasional use at slack periods or when distributors had prestigious films (such as adaptations of Shakespeare) that were best launched for extended runs in a theatrical atmosphere with separate performances at higher prices.

In the early 1930s, the Academy, Rialto and Cinema House proved that there was an art house market for quality foreign films. The Curzon in Mayfair was specially built to cater for this market – elite in location and programming, it reflected the most modern concept in cinema design.

A new type of cinema was imported from the United States: the newsreel theatre. Inaugurated in 1930 as a change of policy at the Avenue Pavilion in Shaftesbury Avenue, the short programme of news, cartoon and 'interest' films proved so popular that from 1934 onwards News Theatres were specially constructed to tap this market, often shoehorned into awkward basement spaces or (in the case of the Victoria Station News Theatre) erected on stilts.

The first big new West End cinema for more than seven years was on the very fringe of the West End, the Paramount at Tottenham Court Road. Quite why the Paramount film company opened this very luxurious cinema to supplement its two centrally-located ones (the Plaza and Carlton) is not clear, but its location was soon to prove a handicap.

Cinemas with a firm repertory policy were also catching on, and the Classic at Baker Street was purpose-built to revive popular films, the flagship of a chain of cinemas dedicated to the policy.

For many years, the national exhibition scene was dominated by the Gaumont and ABC circuits. But in 1937 Oscar Deutsch's rapidly-expanding Odeon circuit demonstrated its determination to rival if not overtake them with the opening of a vast new Odeon in Leicester Square, which with its huge tower and black exterior was the West End's most conspicuous cinema and a compelling advertisement for the entire chain. Neither of the competitors had anything to match it in size, location or profit potential: ABC had only the Regal out at Marble Arch and the small, old-fashioned Rialto (no longer an art house), while Gaumont was at least numerically strong with the smallish Haymarket house bearing the circuit name, plus the Tatler, Marble Arch Pavilion, Movietonews Theatre (former Avenue Pavilion), Dominion, Tivoli, New Gallery, and outlying New Victoria.

The last major addition to the West End scene was the Warner in October 1938, just off Leicester Square, built to showcase the films of Warner Bros.-First National. Together with the Odeon, the Warner confirmed Leicester Square as the very heart of filmland. These cinemas, along with the older Empire and Leicester Square Theatre, played major first runs and this inevitably weakened the position of other West End houses. The Dominion, Astoria and Tivoli were among the cinemas that suffered, having to play second-runs or premiere weaker films.

□□□□

The West End had reached virtual saturation point by the time the Second World War had begun, besides which the high cost of sites deterred further expansion. One scheme that might have come to fruition in the West End was the cinema planned as part of the redevelopment of the Haymarket Stores site at the corner of Haymarket and Coventry Street. Announced in January 1939, this would have been a 500-seater designed by Edward A. Stone and specialising in foreign-language pictures. Work was supposed to start around March 1939. Also, in February 1939, plans were passed for the conversion of Princes Restaurant at 196 Piccadilly into a cinema.

□ **London's West End in 1936, with the Plaza Piccadilly Circus strikingly outlined in neon in the background** *(ph: G.W.C. Taylor, A.R.P.S.).*

(The Princes had been used for occasional special film shows while a restaurant, as on a Sunday in January 1909.)

Only two West End cinemas, the Gaumont News Theatre (former Avenue Pavilion/Movietonews Theatre) and the new Embassy Tottenham Court Road, were destroyed by enemy bombing, but many others closed for various periods because of damage, lack of business, or shortage of worthwhile films. The safe arrival of new prints of major films from Hollywood was a matter of note (many prints were lost at sea), and undoubtedly the arrival of big pictures like *Gone with the Wind* helped boost Londoners' morale.

After the war, West End cinemas prospered for a few years, but by 1950 London-area audiences seemed to be favouring local venues. There was always a delicate balance between the West End and the suburbs. The West End had its special ambience and provided the first chance to see new films, but counting against it were much higher admission prices, travelling costs (for anyone not working in the West End), and (in most instances) shorter programmes (as contrasted with the double-bills at local cinemas). The Empire attempted to lure audiences with a stage show along with the big screen attraction, hoping to establish itself as London's answer to the Radio City Music Hall, but its restricted access to new films and the high cost of live shows brought an early end to the policy.

As attendances plummeted in the 1950s, some cinemas like the Marble Arch Pavilion, the New Gallery and the Tivoli, once West End leaders but now marginal, were sold off for redevelopment. Sites were becoming too valuable to be occupied by cinemas alone. When a new cinema was included on the site of

the former Avenue Pavilion/Gaumont News Theatre in Shaftesbury Avenue, it was tucked away in the basement. This was not an original concept, as the Ritz Leicester Square and some news theatres had been located below ground in the 1930s, nor was it unsuited as cinemas did not require windows and daylight; but it did result in their street presence being diminished. This was particularly true when the former Gaumont Haymarket was replaced with a basement Odeon having a miniscule foyer.

In the Sixties, the West End was home to many roadshow attractions, epic films shown on giant screens that with stereophonic sound overwhelmed the spectator, providing an experience that local cinemas could never match when they belatedly played ordinary prints of the same films. Cinerama spread from its original base at the Casino to the Coliseum and Royalty Theatres; other huge screens for rival systems like Todd-AO, Cinemiracle and D-150 occupied the Metropole, Astoria, Dominion, Odeon Tottenham Court Road and the new Odeon Marble Arch. Only the latter still retains a vast screen for 70mm presentations, a facility that has never been properly exploited, although the Empire, Odeon Leicester Square, and Warner West End can still mount an impressive display.

Both the Odeon Marble Arch and the Empire are reduced versions of older, larger cinemas. At the Empire, a new cinema was fashioned out of the old balcony area while a dance hall was constructed where the stalls had been, and at Marble Arch a new Odeon was built over shops while an office tower was included at the rear of the site. Similarly, the old free-standing Curzon in Mayfair was replaced by a modern one with several floors of offices overhead.

Even when cinemas retained their size, owners often felt impelled to give them a new image by modernisation. In this way the Odeon Leicester Square lost its glorious 1937 interior, and the Leicester Square Theatre lost its theatrical trimmings to become a bland shell.

At least they have space. Elsewhere, claustrophobic new mini-cinemas were purpose-built as at the Cinecenta Panton Street and Swiss Centre Scenes, and already small former news theatres were divided down the middle to form two screens at Piccadilly Circus and Baker Street.

Today, Leicester Square is more than ever the heart of filmland, with the current Empire and the Odeon as the two most prestigious mainstream cinemas in the West End. The cinema area has become increasily more concentrated around Leicester Square and its immediate environs in the last thirty years, after having once spread far and wide along the Strand and up Kingsway, along Regent Street to Oxford Circus, and up Tottenham Court Road to Warren Street.

As this book demonstrates, London did have many glorious cinemas, and the

Empire of 1928 and the Odeon Leicester Square in its original form were the most impressive. Had either survived intact, they would now be spectacular attractions in their own right, regardless of the particular films on the screen.* Unfortunately, there is no great picture palace left in central London to match its magnificent array of live theatres. (Of course, the New Victoria survives: but not as a cinema, and damaged within and without, lacking its underwater atmosphere inside and now rather characterless outside.)

There is one small gem still standing, the Rialto in Coventry Street, but that has been cocooned from public view for nearly a decade and its chances of becoming a cinema again are extremely poor. We British may cherish our live theatres, but we have yet to learn to appreciate our picture palaces. Look at the illustrations on the pages that follow. Did we have to lose quite so much of this splendour?

The West End cinema scene continues to change dramatically. In one week in 1990, six screens were lost when the Cannon Moulin closed. A week later, five new screens were opened at the Odeon Mezzanine in Leicester Square. As the six old screens showed sex films and the five new ones show mainstream fare, this was a gain of sorts – yet one of the sex film screens had been a cinema since 1910 and had actually altered little, while the new sextet only earn respect for the ingenuity with which they were crammed into the space they occupy. At the time of going to press (April 1991) there were plans to rebuild the Warner behind the existing façade to create a modern seven-screen complex. And four

* There might have been others. The records of the American architect C. Howard Crane indicate that he was, at one time around the late 1920s, lined up by movie magnate William Fox to design, as part of an international expansion programme, a Fox Theatre in London (no location given) which would certainly have been on a massive scale, perhaps comparable to his celebrated Fox Theatres in Detroit and St. Louis. And Crane was also involved in one astonishing scheme in the early to mid-1930s that would have provided a London version of New York's Radio City, to have been built at Hyde Park Corner on the site of St. George's Hospital and of houses along Knightsbridge. This included a 6,000-seat equivalent of the Radio City Music Hall for films with stage shows, plus an opera house seating 3,350, and a large café. Coloured sketches of the grand foyer and auditorium of the proposed London music hall show marked similarities with what had been built in New York. Many of the same architects were involved, with the addition of C. Howard Crane, and it seems that the legendary showman Samuel "Roxy" Rothapfel also participated in the scheme. Only an album of drawings and some plans survive, now in the RIBA Drawings Collection. For an article about the scheme, see "A Vision in Vitrolite" by Jill Lever in *Country Life*, 14 November 1985.

new cinemas seating 1,800 are scheduled to open high up in the Trocadero Centre, once to have been the West End base for fresh competition from Canadian exhibitor Cineplex Odeon but now to be further additions to the Cannon chain (this scheme had promised five screens seating up to 2,500 in December 1987).

This and existing Cannon cinemas are likely to take the name MGM or Metro Goldwyn Mayer Cinemas following the parent Pathé company's acquisition of MGM/UA in America in early 1991 (already, all Cannon cinemas display the lion logo and Metro Goldwyn Mayer name on their entrance doors).

This, then, is the history of London's West End Cinemas to early 1991. Cinemas are listed in their order of opening but can be quickly found by consulting the index at the back of the book. We have dealt with simple additions of new screens to existing cinemas, straightforward subdivisions, and ordinary reconstructions as extensions of the history of the original cinemas. But where buildings were completely demolished for cinemas to be rebuilt or where cinemas were completely repositioned within existing structures or were otherwise (like the current Empire) totally different inside and out, then we have treated them as new cinemas.

We have included the serious club cinemas (many in an appendix at the end) and one or two of the more prominent sex film clubs but in general we have excluded the porno sites, as well as the numerous private preview and editing theatres in the area, and other private cinemas like that of BAFTA in Piccadilly.

We are well aware than much fuller stories could be told about cinemas covered – especially about their managers, organists and staff – and some longer articles have already appeared in the magazine *Picture House* on the Odeon Leicester Square (in issue 11, Winter 1987/88) and the Empire (issue 13, Summer 1989). We are also aware that not all the cinemas in this book are adequately covered pictorially, but we have been unable to locate illustrations of, for example, the Academy's auditorium before its 1954 reconstruction, or the warm, cocoon-like interior of the Classic Baker Street. If you can put us on the track of further photographs, or feel there is some detail we should have included despite the limitations of space, we shall be more than glad to hear from you.

The CTA

Readers interested in cinemas should join the Cinema Theatre Association, active since 1967 in promoting serious interest in all aspects of cinema buildings. Its bi-monthly *Bulletin* will provide an update on London West End developments and it also publishes an illustrated magazine, *Picture House*, besides arranging visits and lectures. In April 1991, subscriptions were £9.50 annually (£12.00 overseas) payable to Membership Secretary, William Wren, Flat 30, Cambridge Court, Cambridge Road, Southend on Sea SS1 1EJ. Send s.a.e. for further details of the Association.

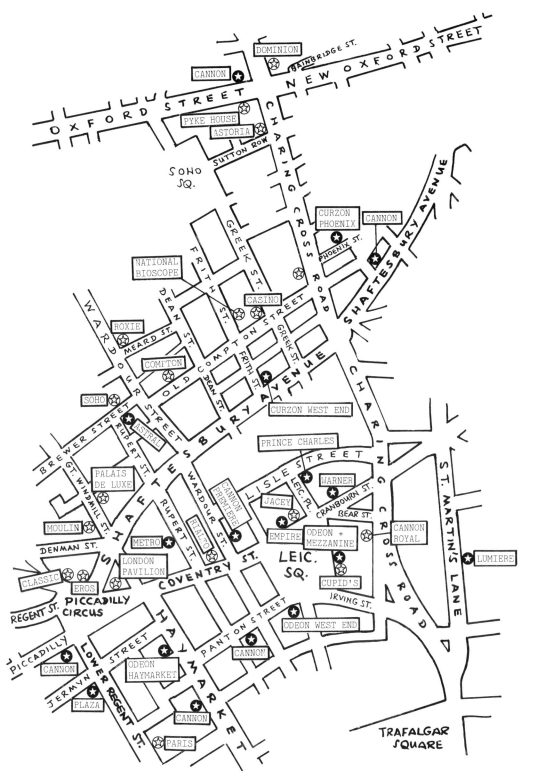

★ cinemas operating in 1991

quarter mile approx.

✪ sites of former cinemas,
cinemas in other uses,
or cinemas closed in April 1991

(former cinemas identified by
their last or best-known name)

⭐ cinemas operating in 1991

✪ sites of former cinemas,
cinemas in other uses,
or cinemas closed in April 1991
(former cinemas identified by
their last or best-known name)

quarter mile approx.

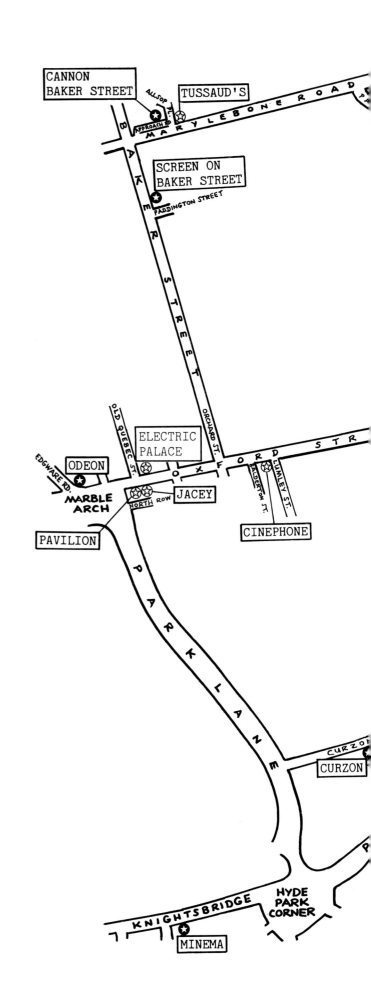

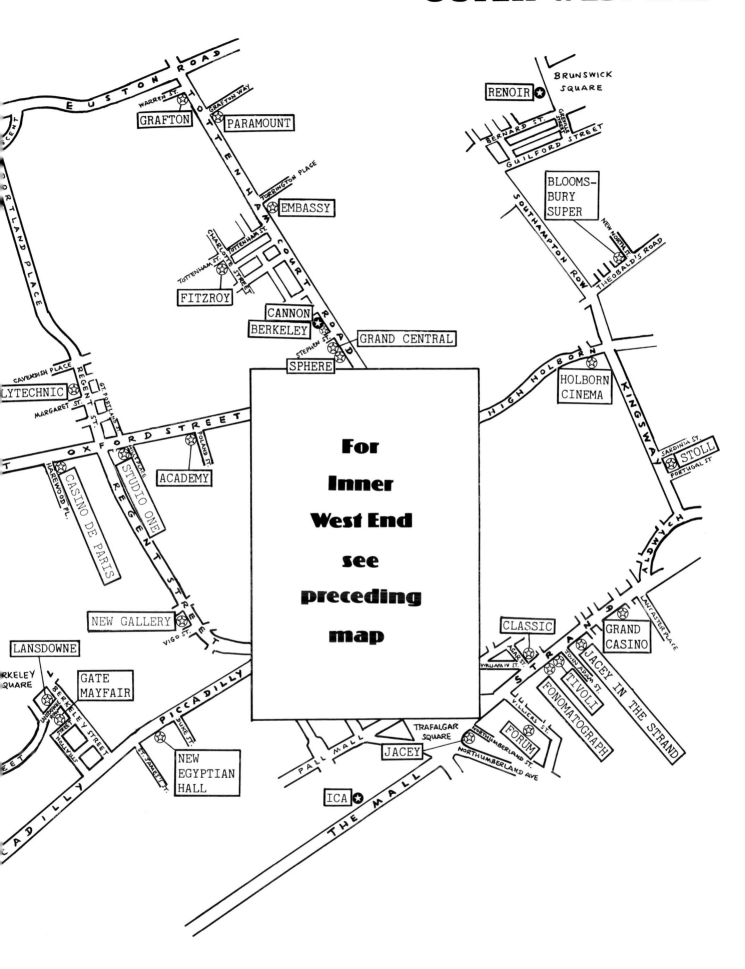

VICTORIA

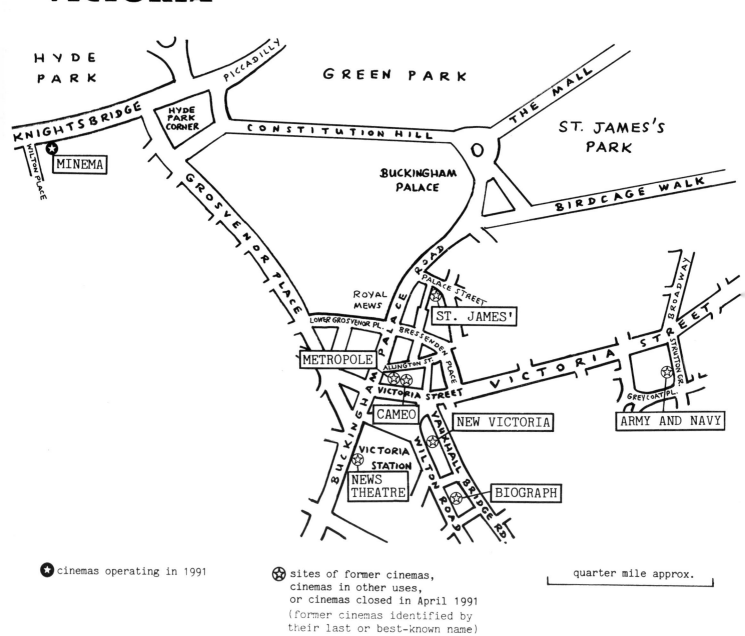

⭐ cinemas operating in 1991

✴ sites of former cinemas,
cinemas in other uses,
or cinemas closed in April 1991
(former cinemas identified by
their last or best-known name)

quarter mile approx.

Circa December 1907
New Egyptian Hall
170 Piccadilly

The original Egyptian Hall was one of the first places to show films. R. W. Paul's Theatrograph was added to the programme of live entertainment from 19 March 1896, making this the third place to publicly exhibit films after the Polytechnic and Empire. It was torn down and replaced by Egyptian House in 1905 but the entertainment tradition was continued when a 123-seat cinema called the New Egyptian Hall was opened in part of the building. This was leased by the Pathé Frères distribution company and attracted a high class of patron, many arriving by motor car. Many visitors to London also attended. Programmes were being changed every day in June 1909 and some patrons were making daily visits.

There was a dainty tea room downstairs furnished in the style of a Japanese tea garden with Oriental lanterns, waitresses in Oriental costumes, and views of the Far East on panels around the walls. Films were shown from 2pm daily and most business may well have been done in the afternoon as higher prices (which included tea) were charged then, all seats being one shilling. In the evenings, admission was only sixpence. Programmes were accompanied by a pianist on a Bechstein

Grand. On Sundays, elevating programmes of art, historical and religious pictures were presented.

In August 1909 the proprietors were doing so well they envisaged using wasted space above the entrance to enlarge the auditorium. However, there was only one exit from the premises and this passed under the projection box, so the London County Council regarded the place as unsuitable for public entertainment. At this time the strongest action the L.C.C. could take was to refuse the premises a music licence and this was done in November 1909. The management declared that it would stay open, even though the piano would be silenced, and that new plans would be drawn up to secure a music licence as well as to enlarge the auditorium and rake the ground floor.

When the new Cinematograph Act became law in January 1910, the cinema was probably compelled to close. It certainly passed to a new management, Picture Entertainments de Luxe, who made structural alterations and were able to re-open it in November 1910. It now seated 180 in stalls and circle, the latter probably being a new addition. The 12ft. by 10ft. screen was built 4ft. behind the proscenium opening so that it was shielded from light in the auditorium and provided a stronger picture. The two projectors had a 78ft. throw to the screen. A Collard

☐ **NEW (or original?) EGYPTIAN HALL**
(courtesy of Tony Moss).

grand piano was provided for the pianists. Tea continued to be provided in the Japanese style, and was included in the higher afternoon admission prices: one and sixpence to the circle, one shilling to the stalls. Evening prices were now one shilling and (for the stalls) sixpence. Programmes were changed twice weekly.

The New Egyptian Hall was licensed under the Cinematograph Act in 1911 and 1912. It then disappears from view. Either it was still unsatisfactory as a place for showing films or the increasing competition had put it out of business. In 1990 Egyptian House still stands and 170 Piccadilly is occupied by the Revelation luggage shop.

☐ **Left, the original EGYPTIAN HALL as the home of the first films, circa 1896.**
Right, the NEW EGYPTIAN HALL and Tea Rooms depicted in 1909 *(courtesy of Tony Moss).*

9 November 1908
Electric Palace
532 Oxford Street

This cinema at the Marble Arch end of Oxford Street was the first of any size in the West End. In 1914, the owners boasted that it was 'The Original Home of Cinema'. In this conversion of a garage with an iron and glass roof, the glass was darkened, the iron supports painted a pretty colour, and a new wooden sloping floor was laid. The promoters were the theatrical impresarios Sedger and Laurillard, and the architect was W. Hancock. There were three exits.

The Electric Palace had 588 tip-up seats on a properly raked floor with boxes on either side at the rear. The auditorium was reached by a lengthy, 30ft. wide vestibule lined by plush divans, flowers and ferns, and quality engravings on the walls. Films were shown in a semi-lit hall rather than in darkness and the way curtains were arranged to shield the screen from the light was the subject of a patent held by the proprietors. In August 1909, four ceiling fans were added to supplement the ones on the side walls, creating a cool atmosphere in summer. Music was provided by a piano and organ. A Japanese-style tea room was added by the end of 1909 and a smoking lounge in January 1910. At some point before 1912, the Electric Palace also acquired a 'handsomely embellished' ceiling.

In January 1909, three months after its opening, a company called Electric Palaces Ltd. was registered to acquire the Electric Palace Marble Arch as a going concern. The company subsequently expanded to run a small circuit of cinemas in the suburbs (Clapham, Cricklewood, Hammersmith, Highgate, Lewisham, Notting Hill Gate, Stoke Newington and Thornton Heath) as well as putting on film shows at the original New Gallery in Regent Street and elsewhere, but went into receivership in 1914-15.

Major alterations were carried out in January 1921 (architect: Gilbert Booth) when the building was extended to add another 176 seats (total now 764) plus space for 66 standing.

In June 1932, with the plush new Regal drawing away custom (as well as the continued competition from the Pavilion across the road), thought was being given to completely rebuilding the cinema. The Electric Palace closed in March 1933 and was demolished to form part of the site for the Mount Royal Hotel.

December 1908
Theatre de Luxe
65 Strand

On premises adjacent to the old Tivoli Theatre (and often thought to be part of it), a firm called Lightning Travels, headed by F. O. Seyd, had established the Tivoli Tourist Station which was a rival to Hale's Tours of the World, presenting moving views photographed along railway lines for an admission price of sixpence. Then one of the first circuits, Electric Theatres (1908) Ltd., took over and created a proper cinematograph theatre which opened around Christmas 1908 with 75-minute shows that changed twice weekly.

The auditorium had an oak-beamed ceiling and the walls were lined with oak and red panelling. It suggested a medieval baronial hall. The floor was thickly carpeted. There were 170 plush red tip-up seats, all priced at sixpence. Films were

☐ **THEATRE DE LUXE, 1910.**

accompanied by a pianist rather than an orchestra but there was the added attraction of a writing room with free notepaper, postcards and envelopes for the use of patrons.

By May 1909 the Theatre de Luxe was opening at 11am daily. Three years later its future was threatened by a road widening scheme for the Strand and it was expected to close in September 1912. However, it was reprieved and went on to house what may have been the West End's first long run—an engagement of at least fifteen weeks of the 5,000ft. feature *Dante's Inferno*, shown daily from 11am to 11pm to the end of 1912 and possibly into 1913. Closure finally took place around the time that the Tivoli was forced to shut for the same road improvements scheme in February 1914. However, because of the Great War, the site wasn't actually cleared until 1922. The new Tivoli cinema eventually opened here in 1923.

December 1908
Victoria Picture Hall
Strand

This cinema opened late in December at the back of the Victoria Arcade next to Terry's Theatre. All seats were priced at sixpence. It was operated by the Sweetmeat Automatic Delivery Company as an adjunct to their penny arcade of automatic novelties which included a mechanical violin. The trade press wondered whether visitors spending their pennies one at a time would be tempted to pay out six times as much for the bioscope entertainment on offer at the rear. The venture was certainly short lived. If nothing else, the conversion of Terry's into a cinema in October 1910 must have knocked it out.

24 May 1909
Electric Theatre
Biograph
47–48 Wilton Road, Victoria

On one wall of the small foyer for at least its last twenty years was prominently displayed a plaque reading:

> BIOGRAPH 1905
> (England's First Cinema)
> Originally called BIOSCOPE,
> the first name for cinema. . .

It is not clear how this totally false information came to be displayed, but the details were accepted as fact and often repeated in print. They may date from 1965 when a press release announcing the theatre's Diamond Jubilee claimed it opened in March 1905, as well as declaring it was the first cinema to be granted a licence under the Cinematograph Act. The occasion was celebrated with a week of special programmes, combining silents (with piano accompaniment) and early talking pictures. Such an apparently notable history gave a rather seedy cinema a distinction it didn't deserve but was, by some definitions, good showmanship.

The Electric was built for Biograph Theatres Ltd., a company formed in 1908 and headed by an American, George Washington Grant. This was the first cinema it opened, having previously acquired five halls that were already operating. The entrance was through an existing row of shops with the auditorium built behind. In typically uncritical but informative fashion, a trade paper report of 17 June 1909 reads: "The latest of the Biograph Theatres, the Electric Theatre, Wilton Road, Victoria, is doing remarkably well, and a good deal better than was anticipated by the most sanguine for the start. The marble vestibule is one of the handsomest in London, and further improved by a number of lovely ferns and plants, and has a floor space of 42ft. by 18ft. and extends with the inner vestibule to no less than 85ft. The theatre has 560 seats in the latest tip-up style, the best seats (6d.) being upholstered in green plush and are situated at the rear of the hall, and being provided with a rise of about 3ft. all patrons can have an uninterrupted view of the large picture (18ft. by 12ft.). The machines (London's latest) are outside the building and behind a wall that varies from 18in. to 2ft. in thickness. In addition to the fireproof gate, in case of accident,

□ **BIOGRAPH exterior and auditorium in 1970** *(ph: Keith Skone).*

there are in the operating-room two kylfyres, two wet blankets, two sand buckets, two water-buckets, and two most efficient operators, Messrs. Alexander and Busting. The hall is semi-lighted but without curtain or shades of any kind. Ventilation is well attended to, three sliding roofs 18ft. by 5ft. being provided. About 4,500 feet of film are given at each performance. A word of praise is due to Mr. Pennington and Miss Moore, who perform at the excellent piano and give some very tuneful and appropriate pieces. The colour scheme is green and red, with a few hanging baskets of flowers as an extra decoration. Ample exits are provided, and more can be cut if needed. Mr. Arthur Bond is the businesslike and genial manager of one of Mr. Grant's best picture theatres."

After a few years, the cinema was renamed the Biograph. In the 1920s, it was operated by Pearl and Saunders, being booked by Harry Pearl.

In 1927, it closed for reconstruction to plans of George Coles. The seating capacity then of 480 was increased to 630 (with standing room for 124) by widening the auditorium (the original width was still indicated by that of the projection box supported by two Corinthian columns). A 20ft.-deep stage with a 32ft.-wide proscenium arch was added, four dressing rooms were provided, the frontage was entirely rebuilt, and a new secondary entrance and exit passage was created, running from doors to the left of the screen through to Vauxhall Bridge Road. The cinema re-opened on Thursday 15 September 1927 with the film *Michael Strogoff* and a live orchestra. Its owners were now the Wilton Cinema company, in which the Hyams brothers were interested, and it operated with three changes weekly of double bills and lower admission prices than the first-run houses like the New Victoria when that opened just down the street, or the Hyams' nearby Metropole.

Talking pictures first came to the Biograph when *Show Boat* was shown on 30 September 1929. Live variety acts were also part of the programme, and apparently were featured for a while even after the Second World War.

It became a struggle to operate cinemas in the Victoria area during wartime (the Biograph apparently lost its offices and staffrooms in the Blitz and was totally closed for a period). The Hyams became anxious to sell their cinema interests and offered the Metropole, Biograph and their Canterbury Music Hall in Westminster Bridge Road to the Odeon circuit in 1943. But Odeon would only take the Metropole and, in order to see that deal completed, the Hyams had to buy out the other shareholders in the remaining two properties, valued at only £16,251, and become sole owners. In time, the Biograph became the last remaining film interest of the Hyams.

The repertory programming at the Biograph provided film buffs with useful opportunities to catch up on old films and it had a large, brightly illuminated

☐ **BIOGRAPH during demolition in August 1983** *(ph: Allen Eyles).*

and well-focussed picture. There was no screen advertising. But the auditorium was barely if at all raked, its seats were tightly packed (the front rows, and perhaps the rest, were without arm rests), and sightlines were bad. It became a gay meeting place with much of the audience constantly moving about, further obscuring the screen. There were problems in renewing the licence. A bouncer was appointed and a notice appeared warning that restive patrons would be ejected.

In time, it became the only cinema still operating in Victoria. It seemed to some that, if it was Britain's oldest cinema, it ought to be 'listed'. As indicated above, the auditorium effectively dated from 1927 and was of little interest, while the frontage had been completely modernised in the early 1960s, so there was no way a preservation notice could have been justified. But, in a manner curiously similar to the overnight destruction of the Firestone building to forestall listing, the Biograph was closed without notice

on Thursday 4 August 1983 after the first day's showings of *Handgun* plus *The Buddy Holly Story*, booked for a three-day run. On the following Saturday, workmen were stripping the roof and the next week demolition began in earnest. It all happened so suddenly that a film programme – *Bronx Warriors* plus *Wrong Way* – was still being advertised in the London *Evening Standard* on Monday, four days after its closure. Disconsolate patrons and curious film buffs were soon to be found wandering around the rubble, which has since been cleared allowing the space to become a 'temporary' car park. On Vauxhall Bridge Road, Biograph House still stands – a small office building built where the former subsidiary entrance stood, with a cinematic emblem carved in stone high up on the side wall.

5 June 1909
Circle in the Square
Cupid's
Palm Court Cinema
28a Leicester Square

The building was occupied by the Cranbourne Club and part of it was converted into a long, narrow cinema providing 198 seats with room for 42 standing. There was a 90ft. throw from a projection box at the side of the vestibule and there were exits onto 19 Charing Cross Road. The architect for the scheme was J. P. Crosby. The Cranbourne Club had a narrow entrance in the middle of the frontage with the cinema entered on the left and exit doors to the right.

Refreshment facilities were an important part of the scheme and a tea-room downstairs seated 300. The original name chosen for the venture was the Bioscopic Tea Rooms but it opened cryptically re-named the Circle in the Square. Its originally intended name became a common nickname for the place.

This was the first full-time cinema in Leicester Square, right next to the Alhambra Theatre where films had been shown in 1896. Audiences were attracted by being able to book seats in advance by telephone. Tea could be taken while viewing the films in the ordinary seats or from an annexe provided with tables. Tea was free to those in the one shilling seats. Films were shown from 2 to 11pm and tea served from 2 to 7pm. Topical events were featured on the screen: a Brighton train disaster was shown the day after it happened in 1910. In January of that year, the Coventry Gallery next door (to the south) was taken over to provide direct access to the popular tea rooms downstairs.

In 1914 the cinema was re-named Cupid's. In 1926 it became the Palm Court but it closed a couple of years later, probably unable to adapt to the coming of sound or to face up to the arrival of the huge new Empire cinema across the square. In recent years, the ground floor has been occupied by an Angus Steak House.

□ CIRCLE IN THE SQUARE, 1913.

7 June 1909
Arena Picture Theatre
Villiers Cinema
Forum
173/4 Hungerford Arches,
Villiers Street, Charing Cross

In the arches underneath Charing Cross railway station, Gatti's Music Hall had been established in 1867. The premises had been disused for many years when they were re-opened in May 1909 as the only boxing hall in the West End. Two weeks later, on Monday 7 June, films were introduced at the Arena for the nights when boxing matches weren't arranged. The alterations to the building were made by the architect W. Hancock. The projection box was installed initially in the balcony which was closed to the public. There was a 90ft. throw to the screen. Puzzlingly high seating figures of as much as 1,800 are given in contemporary reports. Prices of admission were low at threepence and sixpence. Boxing took place on Wednesdays and Saturdays. By August 1909 the proprietors were claiming over 4,000 admissions to the film show on a particular Sunday.

Boxing was phased out and films shown full-time. In 1916, the Arena had only 416 seats and a system of back projection was in use. It was apparently known as the Villiers Cinema from 1918. In 1923 the building was used solely for boxing again, then from 1924 to 1926 it was the Palais de Dance.

On 30 July 1928, following a £30,000 conversion, the place re-opened as the Forum cinema with rear projection and repertory programming. In the Thirties, a combination of continental films and revivals were presented. Some of the foreign pictures were quite sensational: Hedy Lamarr's notorious *Extase (Ecstasy)* and *Bed and Sofa* both premiered here under special L.C.C. licences, having been banned by the Censor.

The Forum closed at the outbreak of war and didn't re-open. It later became an Auxiliary Fire Service depot and then an ENSA depot for cinema equipment. In 1946, it became the new home of the

Players' Theatre, featuring Victorian-style cabaret. The Players' remained in the railway arch until 1987. At the end of that year, the space was excavated as part of the work involved in putting a huge new building over Charing Cross railway station. (The Players' has since returned to better facilities adjacent to its former home.)

□ Members of the West Essex Film Society visit the FORUM, circa 1934 (ph: G.W.C. Taylor, A.R.P.S.).

18 September 1909
Casino de Paris
291 Oxford Street

The Casino de Paris had 175 seats on a raked floor 16ft. wide. The projection throw was 60ft. onto a 12ft. screen. Front seats were sixpence, those at the rear one shilling. Programmes lasted 90 minutes and were shown from 2pm to midnight. Business was noticeably better on Sundays when the Electric Palace at Marble Arch was closed. The cinema was licensed by the L.C.C. in 1911 and 1912 but must have closed as it is not listed after that date and a stationers were in business here by 1916. 291 Oxford Street is occupied in 1991 by a McDonalds fast food establishment.

November 1909
Charing Cross Fonomatograph Theatre
Charing Cross Electric Theatre
Charing Cross Cinema
53 Strand

An amusement arcade with automatic machines had been established here by Pastimes Ltd. when the premises were taken over by Novel Electric Theatres Ltd. and converted into a cinema to hold 180 patrons which was opened in the middle of November 1909.

The 85ft. long auditorium was particularly narrow but the floor was raked. The most expensive seats, price one shilling, were in the centre beneath an oblong glass dome with ventilating fans at each end. Other seats at sixpence were located at the front and back. Back projection was used and had several advantages. It used less electricity; there was a good picture even when daylight was streaming into the auditorium from vents and open exits; and it was well isolated from the audience in case of fire. Tea rooms, a café and a ladies' salon were located over the entrance hall and part of the auditorium.

In 1910 ninety minute shows were offered from 2 to 11pm. By June 1911 the cinema had changed name from the cumbersome Fonomatograph Theatre to Electric Theatre and programmes were changed daily. Although there is a suggestion of a fire, closure around 1922 was more likely caused by the Strand road-widening scheme that claimed the nearby Tivoli.

4 December 1909
Gaiety
Sphere News Theatre
28 Tottenham Court Road

The Gaiety was the first of a great number of cinemas that would open in close proximity at the southern end of Tottenham Court Road. The architect was H. M. Theobald. All 240 seats were priced at 6d. and there was a 50ft. throw to the screen. After talking pictures arrived, the Gaiety reputedly became the last silent cinema in London.

In 1931 the building was extended at the rear to reach Tudor Place and 94 extra seats were added. Then in 1933 it was totally reconstructed to plans of Alister G. MacDonald, reopening on Monday 20 February as the Sphere News Theatre. It was a long, narrow theatre with concealed lighting in two linear troughs in the ceiling as the most striking feature; there were three spheres in low relief representing ringed planets high on each side wall. There were now 238 seats. The promoter was Max Feldman who later formed the Monseigneur circuit with Jack Davies. The Sphere became part of the group and the circuit booking office was established here.

The Sphere was closed by bomb damage in September 1940 and never re-opened. Some years later the building was adapted to shopping use and finally demolished in 1975 for the huge redevelopment scheme on the west side of Tottenham Court Road that has the new Cannon three-screen cinema at the other end.

Circa December 1909
Jardin de Paris
6 Ingestre Place, Soho

A certain F. Haté, who ran the Haté Film Cleaning Company at 8 Ingestre Place, seems to have opened his electric cinema theatre, also known as Haté's Cinema, as a sideline, geared for the ordinary workers of Soho. The cinema was certainly open by Christmas 1909. Mr. Haté also started a school called the Situations Bureau in the summer of 1910 to train operators who could gain practical experience in his cinema.

Plans were drawn up in 1912 for a new 240-seat cinema (architect: R. H. Kerr) at the same address (with standing room for 60 more patrons) but it is not known whether the re-building ever took place. In any case, the cinema here closed circa 1916. Today, the cinema's entrance on the right-angle corner is occupied by exit doors from a large garage which has been built in its place.

December 1909
Madame Tussaud's Cinema
Marylebone Road, Baker Street

There was a large, little-used ground-floor dining hall below the Grand Hall in the ten-year-old new north wing that in 1909, just before Christmas, was converted into a cinema as an added attraction for visitors at no extra charge. Hour-long shows were presented throughout the day. 300 seats were provided and those at the back could be reserved for threepence. Tussaud's were still advertising "Free displays of topical moving pictures" in December 1920 but not after that, so shows may have been discontinued. In any case the cinema was destroyed by a fire in 1925. It was replaced by a new Madame Tussaud's Cinema (see 1928).

☐ **SPHERE NEWS THEATRE, 1933.** *(Interiors and night exterior courtesy of* **The Architects' Journal,** *ph: Sydney W. Newbery).*

Circa 20 December 1909
Palais de Luxe
Windmill
17/19 Great Windmill Street

The Palais de Luxe was the first of two cinemas to open in this short street, both of them conspicuous from Shaftesbury Avenue at its foot. In *We Never Closed*, Sheila Van Damm describes the building: "From the outside it was an Edwardian wedding cake fantasy, tier upon tier of stout, elaborately projecting cornices and ledges of grubby white stone ascending around windows to a height of five floors above the Great Windmill Street pavement, and proudly surmounting the whole design, for no reason I can think of except that the architect was a romantic soul fond of castles, were twin turrets, elegantly domed." It may well have been a pre-existing structure into which the cinema was inserted.

Patrons were offered free tea between 4 and 6pm and free coffee between 7 and 9pm. The one shilling rear stalls were stepped for a better view. The front stalls were sixpence. In 1914, a capacity of 600 was claimed. The Palais de Luxe was extensively improved early in 1916 and remained a cinema until the late Twenties, turned into Britain's first art house by Elsie Cohen for its final year.

It became the Windmill Theatre on 22 June 1931 after alterations (architect: F. Edward Jones) which included the construction of a windmill-shaped frontage. It had a shaky start as a legitimate theatre and films briefly returned in the autumn of 1931 in an unsuccessful art house policy. It then entered its most famous phase as a comedy and striptease house from 4 February 1932, becoming one of the few attractions to stay open throughout the war, and lasting until 31 October 1964.

The Compton group turned it into the Windmill cinema from 2 November 1964 with *Nude Las Vegas*. It had 320 seats. It was taken over by Classic in May 1966 during a lengthy secondary run of *Darling* and in 1968 was throughly modernised with drapes everywhere. It closed on 9 June 1974 with *Sex of Their Bodies* and *Love-Hungry Girls*, having been sold to girlie-show impresario Paul Raymond. In 1984, it was La Vie en Rose Theatre Restaurant. In 1986, it became Paramount City, featuring live entertainment, including series recorded for TV.

☐ **Entrance to PALAIS DE LUXE seen in frame enlargement from an unidentified film. Note advertising of major stars Mary Pickford, Mary Miles Minter and Pauline Frederick.** *(From BFI Stills, Posters and Designs collection.)*

12 February 1910
Cinema de Paris
Cameo
Cameo Royal
Classic
Classic Royal
Cannon Royal
Bear Street, then 35 Charing Cross Road

This venerable cinema ended its days looking smart, thanks to a thorough refurbishment in 1983 after which it reopened with *Screwballs* on Thursday 18 August. It did not have an ideal layout as the auditorium was entered from doors to the right of the screen rather than from the rear and it had an awkward shape because the adjoining property jutted in to narrow the width of the back part of the single-floor auditorium. Renamed the Cannon Royal on Friday 6 December 1985, it seemed to be doing well with short follow-up runs of films that had opened in bigger cinemas. But with only one screen and nothing built above, it was not making the most profitable use of a valuable site, and it was no real surprise when it closed on 23 June 1988 after a run of *Broadcast News* for a redevelopment scheme.

The side of the auditorium was on Bear Street, occupying most of one side of this short, nondescript passage between Charing Cross Road and Leicester Square. Originally, the entrance to this cinema was on Bear Street, at the back of the auditorium, when it opened on 12 February 1910 as the Cinema de Paris. The architect was W. Hancock. It then had 360 seats (it closed with 311), plus three private boxes and a sliding roof. However, a new and much more conspicuous entrance was created in Charing Cross Road in 1913 (architect for the alterations: Percival Hawkins).

In 1926 the cinema was reconstructed by a leading architect, Robert Atkinson (incorporating decorative plaques by C. F. Aumonier and paintings by T. B. W. Champneys), and it reopened as the Cameo with 476 seats. It was converted from features to a newsreel policy from Boxing Day 1932. Further alterations (that added four more seats) were carried out by the well-known cinema architect George Coles in 1935.

In 1936 it was known as the Cameo Revudenews (presumably a take-off of the .live Windmill Theatre's "Revudeville"), and a separate subsidiary entrance was maintained on Bear Street.

It remained a newsreel theatre until a policy of foreign-language X-certificate films was inaugurated with Brigitte Bardot in *Mam'selle Striptease* from October 1956 when the name was changed to Cameo-Royal and the cinema redecorated in rich hues using patterned wallpaper and royal colours of paint. Since the mid-Thirties, the cinema had been controlled by Clavering and Rose who operated the Cameo-Royal with the accent on titillation and used the Cameo-

☐ CINEMA DE PARIS in 1910, showing entrance on Bear Street and auditorium viewed to rear with boxes at left.

☐ CAMEO in 1926, showing new entrance on Charing Cross Road, other entrance on Bear Street and close-up of exit by latter entrance.

☐ CAMEO as a news theatre in 1931 and during war (when it seems to have been temporarily an amusements centre offering a rifle range and darts) (note tower of Odeon Leicester Square in background).

□ Above, as CLASSIC in May 1977 and as CLASSIC ROYAL in January 1984 *(both ph: Keith Skone)*.
Below, auditorium in 1984 with Cannon circuit logo on carpet *(both ph: Allen Eyles)*.

Poly to present more up-market attractions; but occasionally quality films of mixed market appeal like *Onibaba* and *Une Femme Mariée* would play at the Cameo-Royal.

Classic Cinemas acquired the Cameo circuit from Clavering and Rose in September 1967. The cinema was renamed the Classic Royal on 14 April 1972, plain Royal (from 1 December 1977) and Classic Leicester Square *(sic)* from 11 January 1979. Up until 31 July 1983, the cinema had been the only home of all-night shows (held every night) in the West End; but these were discontinued when the cinema closed for its refurbishment on 7 August. At one time, there had been plans to build further cinemas on top of the existing one and work had even begun on constructing a second projection box. But the only income that was derived from all that valuable space above the cinema came from an advertising hoarding that had earlier promoted the cinema and its attractions.

The Cannon Royal was demolished in February 1989, and a new, much taller office building with ground-floor retail space on Charing Cross Road has replaced it, called Cameo House.

12 February 1910
Grand Central
Bijou
Cineclub 24
24 Tottenham Court Road

Opened on the same day as the Cinema de Paris and only two doors away from the Gaiety, this was a long, narrow hall with 395 seats on one floor (only 41 had arm rests); it widened out towards the screen on the left halfway down, and had a single central gangway. The first proprietors of the Grand Central were Walter Hyman and A. D. Rosenthal whose architect was Keenes Purchase.

There was a projection throw of 138ft. which was considered immense at that time. It was claimed that a 5ft. rake ensured a clear view of the screen from every seat. There was considerable standing space at the back. A sliding roof helped cool the theatre during the summer heat. A pianist accompanied the films.

Prices of admission were only threepence and sixpence, with the best seats in the middle. A pot of Lyon's tea and a piece of cake were given to all patrons attending between 4pm and 6pm. The Grand Central was open from noon to 11pm. Competition was so intense (or disorganised?) that in 1912 it was playing the same film as the Gaiety almost next door. During 1922, an orchestra of violin, cello and piano was promoted to playing daily instead of three times a week.

In time the Grand Central gave its name to a small circuit of cinemas that principally included the larger Majestic and Carlton just up the road on the same side of Tottenham Court Road. In May

□ BIJOU, 1928 (courtesy of Kevin S. Wheelan).

1928 the cinema was re-named the Bijou. In August 1929, a proposal was made to put up a 3,000-seat super cinema in place of the Bijou and Carlton. The other Grand Central halls passed into other hands and the Bijou closed circa 1931.

The premises were put to retail use, then rather surprisingly made a filmic comeback in 1969 when the expanding Cinecenta group re-opened the building on 11 September as Cineclub 24 with the sex film As the Naked Wind from the Sea for club members only. There were 250 seats and the venture lasted until 24 December 1976 when redevelopment finally came to this section of Tottenham Court Road, claiming not only the Bijou and former Carlton (now Berkeley) but the former Majestic (now La Continentale) as well.

17 February 1910
Pyke House
Cinematograph Theatre
Phoenix
19/23 Oxford Street

This cinema was the main feature of a development at the eastern end of Oxford Street facing the old Oxford Music Hall which also included a shop linked to the lofty basement and four floors of offices served by a lift. Facing the building, the entrances to the offices and shop were to the left while the rest was the entrance to the cinema within a recess that boasted elaborately carved figures in marble above the doors. The auditorium occupied the full width of the site and an exit alongside the screen opened onto Sutton Place.

The ambitious cinema magnate Montagu A. Pyke took a ninety-nine year lease on the entire property in 1909 and opened the cinema as the fifth on his circuit. It seated 350 people (500 was originally claimed) and had a shallow balcony with steeply stepped rows of seats, which curved forward at each side. The seating throughout was of Hampton's finest brocaded green silk and gilt-framed tip-ups and the price of admission—sixpence, one shilling, two shillings—reflected only the position of the seat.

This was a lavishly appointed cinema for its time, though obviously tight for space. With the crash of Pyke's circuit (Amalgamated Cinematograph Theatres Ltd.) in 1914, the cinema passed to other

□ PYKE HOUSE CINEMATOGRAPH THEATRE, 1910.

hands and was renamed the Phoenix. It closed for six months in 1919, reopening in January 1920 after the interior had been renovated and new indirect lighting installed. It closed circa 1925.

In his reminiscences ("When I Was a Cinema King", *Picture House*, No. 10, Spring 1987), Pyke recalled: "One of the disadvantages of the Oxford Street cinema was that in those days Messrs. Crosse & Blackwell's factory used to back on the alley behind it. When walnut pickles and similar activities were in progress of being made, the smell was sometimes so nauseating in the cinema that women nearly fainted and strong men deserted their seats". The offending factory would in time become the Astoria cinema.

According to Pyke, he had only been able to open a cinema here by building it in such a way that, if it failed, it could easily be converted to other uses. By the early 1930s, the premises had become Smart's furniture showrooms. In the 1980s, the ground floor has been used as a Claude Gill bookshop while the Regent School of English has occupied the first floor.

☐ **PYKE HOUSE CINEMATOGRAPH THEATRE, 1910.**

5 March 1910
Piccadilly Circus Cinematograph Theatre
Piccadilly News Theatre
Centre News Theatre
Cameo
Cameo Moulin
Classic Moulin
Moulin Complex
Cannon Moulin Complex
44 Great Windmill Street

"On Thursday evening last," Montagu Pyke told a trade reporter in late November 1909, "I decided to take over the picture show that was to be opened in Great Windmill Street, Piccadilly Circus. I returned to the office and caused a letter, enclosing a stamped telegraph form, to be sent to my shareholders, and before eleven the next morning, the whole of the amount was subscribed, and here are the cheques that bear out my statement." Cheques from £25 to £1,000 were shown to the scribe.

And so the Piccadilly Circus Cinematograph Theatre opened as the seventh in the Pyke circuit and the second in the West End. It was to have been called the Electric Pavilion and the original architect was H. Harrington. After his plans were rejected in November 1909, Pyke had his regular architects Gilbert and Constanduros draw up new plans which were approved the following month.

The cinema survived Pyke's financial collapse in 1914. Its capacity in early days was stated to be 300 (on one floor). At the beginning of the Thirties, it became one of a rash of news theatres and continued to offer a programme of this type until 1961. After the war it had become one of Clavering and Rose's Cameo circuit with an appropriate change of name. Following redecoration it re-opened as the Cameo Moulin on 16 November 1961 with a policy of sexy 'X' films. 'Moulin' being French for windmill, the name was obviously inspired by the famous theatre across the road.

The cinema became the Classic Moulin in 1972 (the Classic circuit had taken over the Cameo group in September 1967). Four additional cinemas were added in adjacent areas to form a five-screen complex which opened on 28 April 1977. The old auditorium was unaffected and remained open during the construction work. Seating figures were (1) 250 (the original cinema); (2) 137; (3) 119; (4) 100; and (5) 81. These all showed continuous double and triple bills of certificated sex films at a bargain price (£2.50 in 1984, £3.50 in 1990), opening around 11.15am in 1990 (Sundays from 1pm) with late shows every night. In November 1985, the Dilly cinema at 41 Great Windmill Street became the Cannon Dilly but soon lost its separate identity, becoming a sixth screen at the Moulin Complex. Though part of the Cannon Classic circuit (later just Cannon), the

□ Above, as MOULIN COMPLEX in 1984 *(ph: Keith Skone)*.
Below, auditorium as PICCADILLY CIRCUS CINEMATOGRAPH THEATRE in 1910.

14 July 1910
Cinema House
Studio One
Studio 1·2·3·4
225 Oxford Street, Oxford Circus

Melville S. Ward was the architect of Cinema House which had an auditorium in Jacobean style with panelling throughout in old oak. There were 500 seats on the raked ground floor and 100 seats in the cantilevered balcony. It was open from 12am to 11pm with two changes weekly. A restaurant was an added attraction from 1912. Prices of admission in 1910 were stalls sixpence and one shilling, circle two shillings.

The cinema had a narrow and tall frontage with several floors of offices above the entrance and auditorium. Originally rooms were set aside for developing and drying news film that could then be projected onto the screen.

In the early Thirties Cinema House had become an art cinema, operated (like the Academy further along Oxford Street) by Eric Hakim. Then in the spring of 1934 it was acquired by the D. J. James circuit. Soon plans were drawn up to convert the large basement area (which had been used as a restaurant) into a second cinema, and Cinema House closed in the autumn of 1935 to enable building work to go ahead beneath the auditorium. No substantial alterations were made to the appearance of the existing cinema.

On 7 March 1936 gala premieres took place simultaneously starting at 8.45pm. to re-open the old cinema and introduce the new one. Cinema House was now known as Studio One and resumed its foreign film policy with Annabella in *Eve of Battle*. The new auditorium was known

□ Drawing of CINEMA HOUSE published in August 1910.

complex was advertised separately from the rest of the group.

It was long intended to enlarge the site and make it a 14-screen multiplex, no longer showing sex films, with the additional screens being built further up Windmill Street. But in 1990 Cannon declared that safety requirements had reduced the seating capacity to a point where the scheme was no longer viable. By this time, 'adult' cinemas were becoming a thing of the past: new sex films were no longer being issued to cinemas and much of the audience was now watching them on video at home. The

Cannon Moulin Complex closed very abruptly on Tuesday 10 April 1990. For the record, the final attractions (all 18 certificate) were (1) *American Girls in Heat* plus *Women of Pleasure* plus *Sweet Body of Bianca*; (2) *Puss and Boots* plus *Blue Emmanuelle* plus *Natalie*; (3) *Swedish Playbirds* plus *Come Make Love with Me* plus *Country Nurse*; (4) *Private French Lessons* plus *Sex Express* plus *Sex in Sweden*; (5) *Young Emmanuelle* plus *Love, Lust and Ecstasy* plus *Blonde and the Black Pussycat*; and (6) *Misbehaving* plus *Desires Within Young Girls* plus *Sweet Sexy Savage*.

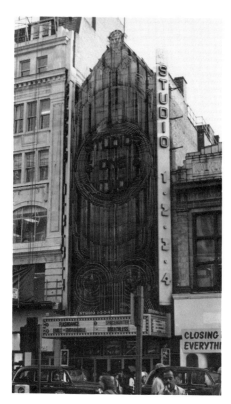

Studio Two was re-named Studio 4. The four cinemas often shared in first-run attractions and were well located to draw in shoppers at Oxford Circus.

But Star preferred to realise the value of the site and closed the complex on Saturday 8 December 1984 with *Conan the Destroyer* in 1, *The Bounty* in 2, a double-bill of *Maîtresse* plus *Last Tango in Paris* in 3, and *Romancing the Stone* in 4. The auditorium, which had a side wall on Hills Place, was replaced by offices entered from this side street, while the entrance hall has become a Benetton shop. All the old neon above the entrance (long disused and left there falling to pieces) was removed and the frontage restored to its plain original appearance above street level.

as Studio Two and operated as a newsreel theatre (see under 1936 for further details). A simple neon display was introduced outside. These were the West End's first twin cinemas, served by a single central paybox.

Studio One was described in a trade paper of the mid-Thirties as "the distinguished temple of Continental screencraft". In advertising it emphasised "No connection with any other Continental Cinema in London". It closed temporarily in early October 1940 when air raids curtailed both audiences and opening hours but re-opened on 13 March 1941, when conditions improved, with *Circonstances Attenuantes*, the first foreign film to be shown in London since the previous September. Sadly, it could now advertise as "London's only Continental Cinema".

The supply of European films quickly dried up and Studio One hit upon reviving Walt Disney's *Fantasia* in 1942 which ran

over a year with different French revivals in support. It returned in 1944 and 1945 for further healthy runs and led to Studio One becoming in the Fifties "London's Premier Family Cinema", playing brand new Disney productions and reissues as well as continuing runs of other suitable films like *My Fair Lady*. Foreign films almost entirely disappeared.

On 22 July 1952, the famous tall, intricate, multi-coloured neon sign was switched on for the first time. It is still there but is not used at all.

Disney films continued to premiere at Studio One until 1968 when the two cinemas were acquired by 20th Century-Fox as additional outlets for the company's pictures (it already had the Carlton and Rialto). The Star circuit took over from Fox on 9 December 1976 and closed the cinemas on 30 November 1977 to convert Studio One into a triple operation. This became Studio 1, 2 and 3 with 200, 200 and 88 seats respectively.

15 October 1910

Holborn Cinema
Embassy
210 High Holborn

Holborn had its own small cluster of entertainments as an outpost of the West End. There was already the Holborn Empire music hall. Now came the first cinema, to be followed by the re-opened London Opera House (the Stoll) and the Bloomsbury. The Holborn Cinema was designed by F. W. Foster of Foster & Gill with 335 seats in the stalls and 137 in the balcony (although a different source mentions 50 seats in *two* balconies). The 16ft. by 12ft. screen was set at the back of the stage to exclude extraneous light from the auditorium. The projection throw was 75ft. There were initially three changes weekly and prices ranged from sixpence to two shillings. A tea lounge was on the first floor.

In September 1923 it became the Embassy, with a 75-minute live revue in support of the film. It was adjacent to a celebrated Edwardian eating place, the Holborn Restaurant.

However, by 1925 it had closed and the premises taken over by metal casement makers. Following use by an office equipment company, in mid-1990 the premises were vacant with the building undergoing reconstruction.

☐ **1910 plans for front elevation of HOLBORN CINEMA.**

24 October 1910

Grand Casino
105/6 Strand

Terry's Theatre closed on 8 October 1910 for alterations designed by the ubiquitous W. Hancock and re-opened as the Grand Casino cinema with 900 seats (priced from threepence to two shillings) and six private boxes (two shillings, seating two or three). An orchestra and special effects machine enhanced the films, which were changed initially four times a week. Projection was from a box in the pit. Understandably it was often referred to as Terry's Cinema.

Moss Empires controlled it until 1921 when capacity was given as 500 seats. It was closed on Sunday 3 November 1923 and demolished in road widening. This stretch of the Strand is now occupied by Norman House.

16 November 1910

Corner Theatre
Grafton
134a Tottenham Court Road/ 4 Warren Street

The Corner Theatre was a basement cinema created out of a former wine cellar. The architect for the conversion was William Bennett of Finchley architects Bennett & Stratton and the client was National Theatre de Luxe Ltd. 280 seats were fitted into an awkward shape with room for fifty standing; existing recesses on a side wall were adapted into alcoves for serving tea to another seventy customers. There were two narrow entrances at the above addresses. Programmes changed twice weekly.

In November 1911 the Corner changed hands and was re-named the Grafton. In May 1921 it was principally a second-run house and had booked its programmes ahead to August 1923 (such advance booking being general practice at the time). It closed in 1929 to become the Grafton Theatre the following year, offering "London's Most Intimate Show" until 1940. It was then a BBC Studios for twenty years. A McDonalds fast food restaurant is now situated on the ground floor, using the basement for storage.

20 November 1910
Strand Cinema Theatre
Strand News Cinema
Classic
3/5 Agar Street

This 200-seater opened in November 1910, have been built to plans of Meakin, Archer and Stoneham. Around 1932 it became the Strand News Cinema. It closed for six weeks in 1936 to enable supporting pillars to be removed (architect: Cecil Masey) and general redecoration took place before it re-opened on 26 March. In June 1940 the operating company was described as "hopelessly insolvent" by a judge who ordered it to be compulsorily wound-up.

After the war it became one of the news theatres operated by Capital & Provincial News Theatres Ltd. (who also owned the Classic circuit). Around September 1951 it was renamed the Classic and showed features, changing programmes twice weekly. On Saturday 27 June 1953, after a three-day revival of *Rebecca*, it became the first postwar West End closure. Its ground floor position in what was originally BMA House (later Rhodesia House, now Zimbabwe House) is currently occupied by offices.

1911
Victoria Picture Palace
Wilton Road, Victoria

According to the 1910 plans, this cinema had 498 seats on a single, sloped floor. Its proprietor for many years was E. M. Barker. Alterations took place circa 1925 but it was demolished in 1926, along with adjacent properties, to provide a site for the New Victoria cinema which opened in 1930.

Circa **1911**
National Bioscope Electric Theatre
20 Frith Street, Soho

Little is known about this side-street cinema. It was licensed by the L.C.C. from 1911 to 1914, after which it must have closed. The Samson Film Company occupied the upper floors shortly after that. Today the entrance is occupied by the stage door of the Prince Edward Theatre.

☐ **In this 1910 panoramic shot of Victoria Station forecourt and Wilton Road behind, the frontage of the VICTORIA PICTURE PALACE is indicated by a black pointer.** *(From National Monuments Record.)*

26 August 1911
Pyke's Cambridge Circus Cinematograph Theatre
Super
Tatler
Jacey
Filmcenta
Cannon
105/7 Charing Cross Road

This was the sixteenth and last cinema opened under the direction of Montagu A. Pyke. With 690 seats, it was the largest of his three West End houses. It was soon attracting such a large number of foreign patrons that in 1912 American films were largely discontinued in favour of Continental dramas and comedies. It had a substantial basement which in 1915 Pyke used to store one ton (£65 worth) of waste film until it could be packed and sent to France. An employee soldering a tin-lined box containing some of the film set the whole lot ablaze and perished in the flames on Monday 26 July. Considerable damage was caused to the theatre; a jury delivered a verdict of manslaughter against Pyke and the cinema's engineer, by which time Pyke was already bankrupt.

The cinema was restored and re-opened in August 1916 by West End Cinemas Ltd. as the Super with full orchestra and pipe organ and a claimed seating capacity of 1,000.

In November 1928 the Super was taken over by the recently formed United Picture Theatres circuit which was soon in difficulties and came under Gaumont-British management from July 1930. Following the success of G.B.'s Movietonews Theatre, this was renamed the Tatler from Monday 16 February 1931 and became the country's second cinema specialising in news and shorts. The programmes consisted of a newsreel, cartoon, magazine and two-reel 'interest' (i.e. documentary) subject, changed weekly. The policy was considered so educational that school groups attended as part of their studies. The range of films shown widened towards the end of 1931 to include shorts made by the Empire Marketing Board. For Christmas 1933, an all-Disney programme of Mickey Mouse and Silly Symphonies cartoons was mounted with huge success and continued for several weeks. After UPT tumbled into receivership in January 1934, Gaumont-British acquired full ownership of the Tatler. The provocative American series The March of Time was introduced here in 1935, along with the notable documentary work of the GPO Film Unit, Gaumont-British Instructional and Paul Rotha.

The Tatler was one of several G–B houses used for large-screen television experiments by its subsidiary, Baird Television. In 1938, the Derby was shown live as it happened on the screen via a projection-type cathode ray tube. Subsequently, excerpts from television transmissions were included in the regular programme until a ban was imposed by the BBC later in the year (and lifted once on 23 February 1939 to allow a big fight to be shown).

The Tatler opened a Russian musical comedy The Rich Bride at Christmas 1941, revived a Russian drama Professor Mamlock in January 1942 and then continued to present Soviet features right through to 1947, being supplied (and subsidised?) by the Soviet Film Agency. In 1948 an erratic policy of mainly Hollywood reissues was adopted. In 1949 the cinema was nearly sold to the Monseigneur circuit, and in 1950 it was acquired for £70,000 by Jacey, closing on 13 August.

The new owners reopened it after renovations on 23 September 1950 with the sensational Traffic in Souls, a white

☐ **As the SUPER CINEMA, circa 1929** *(from BFI Stills, Posters and Designs collection).*

☐ As the SUPER CINEMA, circa 1929 (*from BFI Stills, Posters and Designs collection*).

slave drama with an LCC 'X' certificate. After a varied feature policy, the Tatler closed on 21 July 1951 for more 'redecoration' and made a new start as the Tatler News Theatre in October. It continued in the same vein for the next fifteen years, showing more cartoons and shorts when newsreels ceased. Then on 10 February 1966 it became the Jacey and switched to mostly sex films, beginning with *Fanny Hill*. From December 1967 it was advertised as the Jacey Tatler to distinguish it from other Jacey cinemas in the West End.

After it was acquired on a long lease by the expanding Cinecenta group in 1967, it closed on 29 September with *Only in Denmark* and *Red Hot in Bed*, having been a money loser for Jacey for some time. Cinecenta split the building into

three cinemas and reopened it as the Filmcenta on 17 February 1977. *The Gatekeeper's Daughter* opened the 143-seat Screen 1 and *Andy Warhol's Bad* started off the 160-seat Screen 2. These were both downstairs. The former circle was converted to the 141-seat Screen 3 which began life with a sub-run of Clint Eastwood's *The Enforcer*.

These cinemas became part of the Star chain in December 1979 and showed big double-bills of recent popular attractions. After Star's circuit was taken over by Cannon on 30 August 1985, this was renamed the Cannon Charing Cross Road on Friday 6 December of that year (while the Classic Royal further down the same street became the Cannon Royal). Single features became the policy, with occasional new films like *The Good*

Father mixed in among move-overs of popular movies. The three cinemas closed on Wednesday 7 January 1987, with *Big Trouble in Little China, Psycho III* and *Betty Blue* at the last attractions, while in an odd contrast a brand-new single screen cinema, the Curzon Phoenix, was nearing completion immediately opposite. Since then, the building has been converted back into one large space to serve as the new home of the Marquee Club with live music, but virtually no trace of its cinema past remains.

☐ As the TATLER THEATRE showing Russian pictures in Summer 1945.

☐ Television presentation at the TATLER in 1938, showing two Baird projectors (one in reserve) and their operators with small screen set up in front of proper screen tabs.

By October 1911

Court

268 Tottenham Court Road

Where now stands the entrance to the Dominion Theatre once stood the 420-seat Court Cinema. An Italian orchestra started to accompany the films in 1912, and greatly improved attendances. In 1914, it was the central London cinema in the London and Provincial Electric Theatres circuit of ten cinemas (two others were near the West End, in Chelsea and Portobello Road). In 1918, the company was compulsorily wound up by the Board of Trade under the Trading with the Enemy Amendment Act (it was run by a German suspected of signalling to zeppelins from the roof of the Portobello Road site), and the cinemas were sold.

In later years the Court acquired a reputation for showing sex films and closed on a controversial note in March 1928 after showing a daring picture that had been banned by the British Board of Film Censors but passed by the London County Council.

☐ **In this view up Tottenham Court Road in 1912, the COURT CINEMA is behind the bus on the right.**

11 March 1912

Marlborough Hall
Polytechnic Theatre
Cameo News Theatre
Cameo-Polytechnic
Classic Poly
Regent Poly

307 Regent Street

The Marlborough Hall opened in 1912 following reconstruction of the entire Polytechnic to plans of Frank Verity (exterior) and George A. Mitchell (interior) and it was regularly used for specialised film shows, especially wild-life and travel subjects. From 11 April 1923 it was known as the Polytechnic Theatre, having been refitted to seat 630 people in stalls and balcony. In 1927 it underwent another reconstruction (to plans of F. J. Wills) and reopened, seating 610, on March 3 with the notable jungle feature *Chang*.

During the Thirties, film fare was varied but with the accent firmly on edifying entertainment, such as secondary runs of *A Midsummer Night's Dream* and *David Copperfield*. The cinema was leased from the governors of the Polytechnic and had to uphold the reputation of the establishment. In the words of the trade, it was "intellectually select". It was the only West End house not to open on Sundays.

It closed in September 1940, when the Blitz was at its worst and attendances plummeted, to re-open in November with news and interest programmes from 10.30am to 5pm plus the promise of live lunchtime concerts in future. Clavering and Rose added it to their circuit early in the decade and introduced the Cameo name. Foreign films were first tried out when it became the Cameo Continental on 15 November 1947, but it later switched to mainstream revivals, changed twice weekly, as at the Cameo Victoria.

☐ **Below, exterior of Polytechnic in 1921, with entrance to POLYTECHNIC THEATRE at lower left** *(courtesy of Tony Moss).* **Right, auditorium circa 1972 during organ recital** *(ph: John Sharp).*

Some more foreign films were tried and a successful effort to make it into a leading first-run up-market foreign film outlet as the Cameo-Polytechnic began on 9 May 1952 with the opening of *Le Voyage en Amérique*.

The Cameo-Polytechnic (or Cameo-Poly as it came to be known) made a strenuous publicity effort to place itself on a par with the Academy and the Curzon as a distinguished outlet for major foreign films but its highly erratic choice of films and its slightly out-of-the-way location north of Oxford Circus meant that it never really fully succeeded. However, a number of the most notable Continental releases did premiere at the Cameo-Poly—such as *French Can Can*, *Mon Oncle* (shared with the Cameo-Royal), *Les Amants* and *L'Année Dernière à Marienbad*.

Along with the rest of the Cameo circuit, it was taken over by Classic in September 1967 and renamed the Classic Poly from 14 April 1972. It closed on 10 February 1974 to become a live theatre called the Regent, although films were still shown on Sundays and in special seasons. It reverted to full-time cinema as the Regent Poly Theatre from 21 December 1978, was once again called the Classic Poly from 11 January 1979, and closed on 12 April 1980. It has since been used as a lecture hall by the Polytechnic itself.

4 May 1912
Majestic Picturedrome
Majestic
La Continentale
36 Tottenham Court Road

The Majestic Picturedrome (architect: Peter Dollar) was an elegant addition to the busy Tottenham Court Road cinema scene when it opened in 1912. It provided a system of subdued and graduated lighting as the patron passed from the brightly illuminated entrance along a 30ft. deep vestibule into a 45ft. long corridor so that by the time the auditorium was reached the eyes had become accustomed to the gloom instead of being blinded by the sudden darkenss. All the walls and doors leading to the auditorium were panelled in light oak while some 2,020 yards of rich pile Royal blue carpet, embellished with figures of crowns and the monogram M.P., were laid down through the cinema including the entrance.

There were 640 seats, all on one floor, originally upholstered in rose du Barri velvet. In the ceiling was a dome of 60ft. circumference, containing twelve panels depicting angels which were lit up at the intervals. Two Pathé projectors were installed and a policy of first runs only, including some longer feature pictures, was announced. An early attraction was *Exiles in Siberia* with the Russian novelist Max Hunterberg describing what audiences saw.

The Majestic came under the control of Grand Centrals by 1915. They also ran the Carlton/Berkeley almost adjacent, and the two cinemas were always linked thereafter, passing to Eric Hakim's Cinema House c1930 and to Ben Jay in the later Thrities. By this time they were no longer large enough, nor well enough sited, to be leading West End houses, and were independent of any big or influential group.

The outbreak of war early in September

☐ **MAJESTIC PICTUREDROME in 1912.**

1939 closed the Majestic until late the following month. It then closed in late January 1940 until further notice, having been particularly vulnerable to the decline in attendances. Re-opening did not take place until Sunday 25 October 1942 when it offered twice-weekly changes of repertory programmes.

In 1948 Kenneth Rive took over the two halls and after a short closure the Majestic re-opened on 24 April 1948 as La Continentale (on the same day as the Carlton re-opened as the Berkeley). Foreign films, including first runs, became the order of the day.

The two cinemas became the backbone of Rive's Gala circuit, playing many Gala

☐ **Auditorium of MAJESTIC PICTUREDROME circa 1912.**

18 March 1913
West End Cinema Theatre
Rialto
3/4 Coventry Street

The West End Cinema Theatre was undoubtedly the finest of the pre-war central London picture houses. It still stands, hardly altered, but suffering from more than eight years' disuse which has caused much of the plasterwork to crumble away.

The architect was Hippolyte Blanc but all the interior decorations were designed by Horace Gilbert. It was built at a cost of around £31,000 (excluding furnishings and fittings) with a tall, narrow main entrance on Coventry Street leading to an oval-shaped auditorium with a side wall along Rupert Street. The cinema originally seated 452 in the stalls, 232 in the circle, total 684. Four floors of offices were included at the front of the development but they did not extend over the auditorium, while underneath the cinema was the Elysée Restaurant, which later became the Café de Paris, reached by a separate narrow entrance underneath the cinema's canopy.

In 1913 the West End Cinema Theatre made quite an impression externally by the first use of a neon sign in the centre of London: this was a sign that stood out at right angles to the facade proclaiming the cinema's name in red tubular script, while the great window arch was outlined by white tubes filled with carbon dioxide gas. Marble staircases led up to the stalls and circle. A small café was sited halfway up the double-flight staircase to the circle on the first floor landing, behind the tall front window. The rear half of the stalls was raked. Pavilioned boxes were situated to each side of the circle front. With its central dome and richly ornamented plasterwork finished in cream and gold, the cinema had all the elegance of a theatre. It so impressed one American visitor that he used the plans to build a near replica, the Parkway Theatre at Baltimore, Maryland.

The West End was re-named the Rialto from Monday 28 April 1924 and a pipe organ was installed soon after. In the late 1920s, the Rialto was used by the European Film Company, the British subsidiary of Universal, to showcase new Universal pictures.

Once sound came in, it was to be found presenting subtitled versions of European films like *The Blue Angel* (in 1931) and *A Nous La Liberté* (in 1932), styling itself "England's foremost and original Continental theatre".

However, it was converted to a news theatre under Albert Clavering from 27 March 1933—apparently without success since the ABC circuit took it over in

☐ **WEST END/RIALTO Coventry Street.**
Top, exterior in 1954 during 3-D fad (*from BFI Stills, Posters and Designs collection*).
Centre, circle front with box and original decor. Left, circle in 1981 (*courtesy of the Museum of London, ph: John Edwards*).

□ **RIALTO in 1981** *(courtesy of the Museum of London, ph: John Edwards).*

January 1934 and retained it until towards the end of the decade.

The Rialto was under independent control in March 1941 when it was penetrated by a German bomb which exploded underneath the auditorium in the Café de Paris with considerable loss of life. The cinema remained closed until Lou Morris took over, patched it up, and re-opened it on Monday 7 September 1942 with a move-over run from another cinema. Weekly changes were quickly the policy, with Florence de Jong playing the Compton organ which had been installed from the Ritz Sheerness and remained until 1947. The Rialto closed early in January 1946 and was acquired the following August by Alexander Korda's London Films to return to an art house policy.

After a month of repairs, the Rialto re-opened on 29 November with the gala British premiere of *Les Enfants du Paradis* which had a fantastically successful run. The cinema went on to show a remarkably fine selection of new French and Italian films in 1947 and 1948. In 1949 it was leased to a specialised distributor, Films de France, and renovated (architect: George Coles)

before re-opening on Saturday 1 October. *Orphée*, *The Little World of Don Camillo* and *Les Belles de Nuit* were among the films that graced the Rialto's screen, along with the first run of Korda's *Outcast of the Islands*.

In 1954 20th Century-Fox took over the Rialto from London Films. The company had recently launched its new CinemaScope process, was in dispute with Rank, and had determined to premiere films in its own cinemas instead of Rank's West End houses. Fox had already taken over the Carlton and chose the Rialto to act rather as the Ritz did with regard to the Empire. It would be primarily a move-over house to continue runs from the Carlton; but it could play a second print simultaneously; and it could open Fox's more routine or difficult 'Scope pictures that didn't deserve a run at the larger and more prestigious Carlton.

Fox made rapid, extensive but sensitive improvements to their new acquisition over twelve days and nights after calling in Sam Beverley (of Verity and Beverley) as architect. A 25ft. 6ins. wide curved CinemaScope screen was installed slightly in front of the 21ft. proscenium opening within a new arch created from existing

columns and a decorative band across the ceiling, although the top of the old proscenium was visible behind the new swag pelmet. The large boxes to either side of the circle obstructed the view of the larger new screen and were removed with decorative plasterwork being added to harmonise with the existing scheme. Four-track magnetic stereophonic sound was installed with speakers around the auditorium. Redecoration took place in blue, lavender and white. Seating was reduced to 562.

The spruced-up Rialto re-opened on 15 October 1954 with *Three Coins in the Fountain* which had done six weeks at the Carlton. With an ideal location to attract passers-by in the short street between Leicester Square and Piccadilly Circus, the Rialto continued as a popular entertainment centre and Fox carried out further improvements in August 1959 for which the theatre was temporarily closed. This time the architect was Leonard Allen. A huge illuminated advertising panel was erected above the canopy, blocking off the lower half of the big window. Small rotundas that had stood between the entrance hall and the auditorium on both stalls and balcony levels were replaced by wide doorways, with the space gained being used to enlarge the toilets. The old café area on the half landing was reduced to a small waiting space with cloakroom and telephone. But the major change was in the stalls where a reversed rake was introduced in the front half, meaning that the front seats were raised as much as 2ft. 6ins to improve sightlines and the whole floor became a saucer shape in profile. It was possible to restore twenty-two seats removed in 1954 and bring the seating capacity back to 584. A lower platform was built in front of the screen for the display of flowers while the top of the old proscenium arch was removed from view by hanging drapes. A new screen—29ft. 8ins. by 13ft. 7ins.—was erected. A modern ventilation system was installed to replace the old extractor fan, with unsightly new ducts on the rear wall to introduce fresh air.

The Rialto reopened with *Blue Jeans* and remained under Fox control until the company decided to dispose of its British cinema interests in 1977. The fast rising Brent Walker group took it over on 9 March to become their flagship theatre (with Fox initially providing half its programmes). The Rialto became the setting for glittering premieres of Brent Walker productions *The Stud* in 1978 and *The Bitch* in 1979 as well as playing action pictures and revival double bills.

In 1978 the landlords, Electricity Supply Nominees (the pension fund investment body of the Electricity Board), wanted to convert the cinema into a shopping arcade and small theatre (to re-house a fringe theatre on other property owned by the company). Brent Walker called for a preservation order on the historic cinema saying also that "it's very viable indeed" while a spokesman for the Electricity Board declared (according to the London "Evening News") "We want to radically alter it, and restore it to its former glory"—as though the two aims were compatible. Westminster Council promptly rejected the conversion proposal.

Brent Walker's lease was terminated early in 1982 and the Rialto announced "Positively Last Performance 7pm Sat. 9 January", when a revival of *Carrie* was screened before the main feature *Force Five* started at 8.50pm.

Although the Rialto has been offered for let, the asking price was prohibitive for a cinema operator. One scheme to turn it into a restaurant and night club was drawn up but seems to have lapsed. Some income has been derived from letting out the entrance area as a Bureau de Change.

Many attempts had been made since 1977 to have the Rialto officially recognised as an outstanding building, and the only good news since its closure is that it was finally listed in 1989. In mid-1990, notice was served on the Café de Paris nightclub, which had continued to operate in the basement, to enable some sort of redevelopment of the site to take place. We can only hope that the historic gem among London's West End cinemas may yet be restored to public view in some form or other.

May 1913
Army and Navy Cinema
30 Strutton Ground, Victoria

The 1912 plans show the architects as Turner and Javes. The cinema, presumably named after the nearby Army and Navy department store, seated 450 and served the immediate residential area. The programme changed twice weekly in 1918 and later years. The competition at Victoria had increased too much by 1931 and during that year the building became a dance hall instead. This part of Strutton Ground still stands in 1991 but there is no trace of a former cinema in the facade.

□ **RIALTO in 1981: stairs from half landing to circle, and side of theatre on Rupert Street** (*both courtesy of the Museum of London, ph: John Edwards*).

October 1913
Carlton
Berkeley
30 Tottenham Court Road

This part of Tottenham Court Road was becoming saturated with cinemas, what with the Court, Gaiety, Grand Central and Majestic all close by. The Carlton opened as a sister theatre to the Majestic (almost adjacent at number 36) and the two were run initially (and until around 1928) by Grand Centrals. In August 1929, there was a short-lived proposal to build a 3000-seat super cinema incorporating the sites of the Carlton and Grand Central. In later years the Carlton and Majestic were operated by Eric Hakim's Cinema House, then by Ben Jay and others, then finally by Kenneth Rive's Gala. The original 800-seat capacity came down to 650 seats in the 1940s, 602 in the 1950s, and 505 in the 1970s.

The Carlton closed in late October 1939

☐ **CARLTON in 1913 and frontage as BERKELEY circa 1976.**

following a severe drop in business due to war-time uncertainties and curtailed hours and re-opened in May 1943 with programmes of French revivals changed weekly. It then closed for redecoration early in April 1948 and re-opened on 24 April as the Berkeley. Over the years the Berkeley specialised in premieres of foreign films and second runs of British and American hits. Some modernisation took place in 1959 (entrance) and 1969 (auditorium).

A second screen, the 183-seat Berkeley 2, was introduced on 3 May 1973, replacing the former Rectors nightclub in the basement area under the main cinema (much as Academy 2 had been opened in similar space below the main cinema).

The Berkeleys, alas, together with the sister La Continentale (the former Majestic) were sacrificed to a huge redevelopment scheme in which a new triple cinema (taken by Classic) emerged as a replacement. All closed on Tuesday 31 August 1976.

30 May 1914
Marble Arch Pavilion
505 (later 531) Oxford Street

Being built on an impressive scale in one of the best parts of the West End, the Marble Arch Pavilion did much to enhance the reputation of the cinema as a whole. The site at the western end of Oxford Street was once occupied by Tyburn Prison. Camelford House stood there when Israel Davis acquired a lease from the Duke of Westminister to replace it with the Pavilion cinema (which Davis built at the same time as his Lavender Hill Pavilion).

The Marble Arch Pavilion was designed by Frank T. Verity and had 1,189 seats on a single raked floor plus half-a-dozen private boxes and a tea lounge. An organ was placed at the side of the orchestra pit. The cinema had a classical frontage in the form of a loggia. The height of the building was kept low by sinking the auditorium beneath street level.

Evidence of the Pavilion's high reputation is provided by its being the first cinema officially visited by both the King and Queen who viewed the Naval epic *Zeebrugge* there on 10 November 1924. (Eight rows of seats at the rear of the auditorium were entirely removed for the visit by King George V and Queen Mary to make way for three private boxes with ante and retiring rooms, fully furnished. The two chairs occupied by the Royals were displayed in the foyer for many years afterwards.) Another notable occasion was a visit by Valentino in 1925 when riots ensued. Their Majesties returned to the Pavilion with Princess Mary for a Command Performance of *The Flag Lieutenant* on Tuesday 3 May 1927.

Gaumont took over the Davis circuit from 5 June 1927 and Frank Verity drew up plans for the addition of a balcony in 1928 although the work was never done. However, during this year the original Jones organ was replaced by a 10-rank, 3-manual Christie (removed to South Africa in 1948).

In the Thirties the Pavilion more than held its own against the huge new Regal across the road but the focus of West End cinemagoing slowly shifted towards Leicester Square. The Pavilion came to be on the small side and a little remote, taking films on transfer from bigger, more central cinemas. It was one of the Gaumont halls used for big screen television: along with the Tatler, it showed the BBC's transmission of a big fight live on 23 February 1939. The war ended experiments of this type.

The Pavilion stayed open during the war except for a brief period at the height of the Blitz, closing in late September 1940 and re-opening on 10 November 1940 with Hitchcock's *Foreign Correspondent*, moved over from the Gaumont Haymarket. Later in the Forties and early Fifties the Pavilion generally combined with the Gaumont for dual premiere runs.

Then in the Spring of 1952, a

□ MARBLE ARCH PAVILION. Top left, circa 1914. Above, auditorium in 1925. Below left, circa 1948.

distribution company called Archway presented four Italian films at the Pavilion. These were specially dubbed into English in this country in an attempt to widen the market for foreign films. They were successful—one of them, *Behind Closed Shutters*, ran for five weeks, the longest run at the cinema for several years.

This paved the way for Archway to lease the building and run it themselves to launch further dubbed Continental movies. The date of take-over was 2 October 1952. In later years, programming became even more mass-market with dubbed Italian epics like *Theodora the Slave Empress* and *Ulysses* (the latter with Kirk Douglas).

While Archway were running the cinema, the site was sold to Montague Burton (presumably to become the location of a Burton's tailoring shop). However, Archway renewed their lease with Burton's in July 1953 for five years. Then in September 1954 Burton's sold the site. Archway carried on at the Pavilion until 24 March 1956 when it closed with a last screening of *Fire in the Skin* and was quickly demolished to be replaced by a row of shops. These had become a Virgin Megastore in 1990.

1915
(Pathé Frères cinema)
Wardour Street

According to *The Guinness Book of Film Facts & Feats*, a roof-top cinema seating 150 was established by the Pathé Frères distribution company in 1915 in Wardour Street. This was presumably at either 84 Wardour Street where the company had its Hiring Department or at 103/9 Wardour Street where its head office was located. (The same source reveals that the first open-air cinema opened in Britain at Hull in 1912, and that later, in 1917, an open-air cinema was temporarily established in the middle of Trafalgar Square for the benefit of soldiers and sailors on leave.)

☐ **STOLL PICTURE THEATRE. Above, circa 1930. Below, night view circa 1934** *(ph: G.W.C. Taylor, A.R.P.S)*.

31 April 1917
Stoll Picture Theatre
Kingsway

It was Oswald Stoll who re-opened the derelict London Opera House (architect: Bertie Crewe) as the Stoll Picture Theatre on the last Monday in April 1917 and, despite its out-of-the-way location, achieved a legendary success making it into a popular family house. (Films had been shown with variety up to 1913.)

The enormous 272ft. wide frontage was outlined with 3,000ft. of red & and blue neon tubing in September 1932. There were 2,374 seats.

However, increasing competition from new luxury cinemas resulted in the Stoll reporting a year's loss of £2,135 in December 1936. The cinema kept on until the end of September 1940, presenting double features and a stage show, when it closed owing the effects of the Blitz on attendances. When it was re-opened by Stoll on 1 September 1941, revues and musical shows had replaced films. In February 1954, the building seemed likely to become the London home of Cinerama but the Casino was chosen instead. After several stage productions, the Stoll was closed in 1957 and demolished for an office block. At least the developers were forced to include a new theatre, called the Royalty, which was built in the basement with the entrance tucked away on Portugal Street.

3 September 1921
Victory
Bloomsbury Cinema
Bloomsbury Super
114–118 Theobalds Road/ New North Street

It had originally been hoped to open this cinema at Christmas 1912, seating 1,000 to plans of Ernest A. Mann. The Great War and subsequent restrictions on luxury building delayed completion and it wound up costing £85,000 and seating (according to 1920 plans) 1,346 (894 stalls, 452 circle). Victor Peel became co-architect with Ernest A. Mann. The cinema was given the topical name of the Victory and it incorporated three flats, one for the manager.

The Lord Mayor of London declared the Victory open at a Saturday afternoon performance before an invited audience that included 300 wounded soldiers from London hospitals. The first public performance followed at 6pm. The opening attraction was *The Kid*, starring Charlie Chaplin, which was on release all over London that week. The Victory Symphony Orchestra with twenty performers, conducted by Monsieur Meney, accompanied the shows. This was very much a neighbourhood cinema, soon changing programmes three times weekly.

The name was changed to the Bloomsbury Cinema in the mid-Twenties. The London & Southern circuit took it over from November 1929, and operated a repertory policy with low prices, renaming it the Super and slashing prices even further in 1933. An organ by Hill, Norman and Beard had been installed.

The Odeon circuit took over L&S around July 1937 and the Super then seated 918 in the stalls and 455 in the circle, a total of 1,373. It was decided to close the cinema indefinitely because of war-time conditions in November 1940. Within three or four months it had been severely damaged by bombing. Its site is now occupied by Mercury House (Cable and Wireless Ltd.).

☐ **BLOOMSBURY SUPER, circa 1932** *(courtesy of Michael Thomas)*.

April 1923
St. James' Picture Theatre
Palace Street, corner of Palace Place, Victoria

This cinema, down a side street off Buckingham Palace Road, was a conversion from a disused chapel with a new frontage and partial reconstruction inside. It had three changes of programme weekly. With the opening of the much larger, better located and more attractive Metropole and New Victoria cinemas nearby, there was too much competition and the cinema closed on 28 March 1931 to be reconstructed into a

theatre to plans of architect Arnold Dunbar Smith. It re-opened with 603 seats and live repertory performances as the Westminster Theatre on 7 October 1931. Though off the beaten track, it became a lively part of the West End theatre scene and was run for a while (1943-45) by actor Robert Donat. In 1960, the Westminster was acquired by Moral Rearmament and has since been used to present plays and films illustrating the movement's outlook. It has also been booked for commercial stage productions and substantial alterations have moved the entrance around the back.

□ **ST. JAMES' PICTURE THEATRE. Exterior in 1923, auditorium in 1926.**

6 September 1923
Tivoli
65–70 Strand
(corner of John Adam Street)

The Tivoli with its severely simple facade in Portland stone was an imposing building on the Strand for a little over thirty years. It took its name from the old Tivoli music hall which had closed in 1914 for a long-delayed road widening scheme and which had occupied part of the cinema's site (as had an early cinema, the Theatre de Luxe—see 1908).

After the Great War, building restrictions were not relaxed for many years and the new £100,000 super cinema was finally built to plans drawn up by Bertie Crewe and Gunton & Gunton. It had 906 seats in the stalls, 637 in the circle and 572 in the balcony, for a total of 2,115 (there was also standing room for 350 more). Additionally, there were two boxes. A Jardine organ was installed and a Dutch Buffet beneath the entrance hall inaugurated the refreshment facilities which later included a restaurant and two luncheon bars. The theatre drew its water supply from an artesian well 550ft. below the surface. There was a sliding roof over the central dome which could be opened in hot weather. Projection was from the rear of the dome.

In 1925 the Tivoli became the first London cinema to show proper sound films—Deforest Phonofilms. During this year it was taken over by Jury-Metro-Goldwyn, the British branch of what was to become Metro-Goldwyn-Mayer, as a showplace for their new releases. *Ben Hur* and was shown twice daily with advance booking, attracting a total audience of over 1,200,000.

However, when the company had the new Empire ready in Leicester Square, it no longer needed the Tivoli. And so this was taken over by Provincial Cinematograph Theatres early in November 1928, giving that circuit a second West End outlet besides the New Gallery. PCT made some rapid changes over a two-week period—converting a tea lounge to the left of the main entrance into a crush hall for queues, laying down monogrammed carpet, modifying the proscenium arch, replacing the boxes at the sides of the arch with grilles (installing two organ chambers behind one), siting a new Wurlitzer organ in the centre of the orchestra pit, and reseating the stalls and

□ **TIVOLI – the original auditorium.**

reporter sampled conditions in the front stalls. There were still occasional moments of glory—the Queen and Duke of Edinburgh attended the opening night (25 October 1954) of an official Italian Film Festival week when the theatre was hired out—but its days were numbered.

The Tivoli closed on Saturday 29 September 1956 after a week's run of the ABC circuit programme *The Baby and the Battleship* and *Oklahoma Woman*. It had been sold to Montague Burton. Following demolition, the Peter Robinson department store rose in its place; this is now New South Wales House with the Acuman store on the ground floor.

The Tivoli was the first huge West End cinema to disappear, going shortly after the Marble Arch Pavilion. It deserved a better fate. Its Wurtlitzer was saved and could be seen in the 1972 film *Dr. Phibes Rises Again*.

☐ **TIVOLI. Above, auditorium after 1928 alterations. Right, night exterior, circa 1936** *(ph: G.W.C. Taylor, A.R.P.S.).* **Below, exterior in 1947** *(courtesy of Tony Moss).*

circle with 1,553 new chairs (the balcony was taken out of use).

The Tivoli re-opened on 27 November 1928. In December, the PCT circuit passed into Gaumont-British hands. The Tivoli had a huge success with Goldwyn's first talkie, *Bulldog Drummond*, starring Ronald Colman in August 1929. There was a long run of the Eddie Cantor musical comedy *Whoopee!* in 1930, a revival of *Ben Hur* with sound effects in June 1931, and it continued to act as a leading premiere house for films such as *Rome Express* in December 1932. But slowly the Tivoli lost ground to the new super cinemas further west as Leicester Square became the centre of film entertainment. It closed on 25 June 1938 to re-open in August with a policy of second-run programmes changed weekly (as had already become the practice at the Astoria and Dominion).

The declaration of war closed all cinemas for a few days but the Tivoli re-opened only briefly before being shut for an indefinite period from 30 September 1939. It was then severely damaged during a 1941 air raid but its vaults were used as a shelter. Films returned on 22 February 1943 with a premiere run of *It's That Man Again* and a personal appearance by star Tommy Handley on the first night. The Tivoli continued to play mainly first runs, sometimes paired with the New Gallery, until the early Fifties when it was linked with the Astoria playing ABC circuit bookings for a pre-release week directly before they went on their three-leg run through the London suburbs.

In the wide-screen era, the Tivoli came in for sharp and surprising condemnation in the trade press one week when a

11 February 1925
Capitol
Haymarket

The Capitol was the major part of a very expensive (£375,000) development of an island site facing onto the Haymarket and it opened in 1925 with 1,700 seats. It was built for a company run by Sir Walter Gibbons and it established the reputation of its architect, Andrew Mather, whose office was later responsible for a great many Odeon cinemas. The Capitol was leased to the Clavering brothers from its date of opening but they remained in control only until June 1925 when it went back to Gibbons. It became part of General Theatres Corporation when that ill-received circuit was launched by Gibbons and F. A. Szarvasy in March 1928. Gibbons resigned as managing director the next month, and the month after that Gaumont-British took over and installed their own directorate.

The first all-talking British picture, *Blackmail*, had its long premiere run here from Sunday 28 July 1929.* A Norman and Beard organ was played at the interval. A Compton organ was installed in 1930.

In 1935 Gaumont decided to completely reconstruct the cinema by lowering the auditorium to take in the former basement premises of the Kit Cat Restaurant. The Ben Travers farce *Foreign Affaires* was the final attraction and the Capitol closed on Saturday 18 January 1936 to re-open in 1937 as the Gaumont Haymarket.

* *Blackmail* had a single late-night press and trade show starting at 11.15pm on 21 June 1929 at the Regal Marble Arch but did *not* open to the public there.

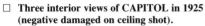

☐ **Three interior views of CAPITOL in 1925 (negative damaged on ceiling shot).**

1 March 1926
Plaza
Paramount & Plaza
Paramount & Universal
Plaza 1–4
17/25 Lower Regent Street/ Jermyn Street

The Plaza was built by Paramount to be its British showcase theatre. The architect was Frank T. Verity and the decoration was by Marc Henri. The cinema has an imposing corner entrance that faces towards Piccadilly Circus—it is surmounted by a dome and tower, the dome decorated in a wavy blue and gold pattern.

This large (1,896 seats) cinema was in the Italian Renaissance style and many genuine antique items of Italian furniture and fittings were included. There was a Royal Circle seating 84 which was reached off the grand foyer. The stalls area below seated 1,138 and the balcony upstairs accommodated 674.

The cost of construction and equipment was £397,639 16s. 9d. Excavation and retaining walls cost £18,573, the main building £265,185 and fees amounted to £12,746. Individual items cost as follows: seating £7,386; Wurlitzer organ £5796 11s 3d.; carpets £4,717; projectors £3,015 1s. 3d.; switchboard (stage) £3,080 10s. 6d.; fixtures £844 15s. 2d.; ticket machines £594; café equipment £511 10s. 5d. Including the site, the total cost of the Plaza was around £500,000.

Opening took place with Dorothy Gish in Herbert Wilcox's British production *Nell Gwyn* before members of the Royal Family. There were live shows in support of the Paramount feature films, and these featured the Plaza Tiller Girls. They were twelve chorus girls, chosen and trained by the Tiller organisation, and noted for their precision. They performed three new numbers each week, seven days a week, and after the evening show jumped into a taxi to appear at East London variety halls. One of them, Peggy Diamond, later recalled: "There were certain basic Tiller steps which I can still remember and they would be re-arranged in a different way. At the Plaza, it was sometimes different as we would have to do something to tie in with the film. There was a film about Russia and they thought it would be a good idea if we did a Russian dance. So we had these rather nice Russian peasant costumes and somebody was brought in to teach us about Russian steps. Then we did hula-hula dances for something about the South Seas". The troupe are recalled in Walter Sickert's paintings "The Plaza Tiller Girls" and "High Steppers" (in the latter, displaying costumes worn for a musical comedy called *Up with the Lark* and the 1929 film *A Little Bit of Fluff*).

In July 1926, shortly after opening, the Plaza had to submit to an injunction not to play its organ and cause noise and vibration which had upset a tenant in the flats at 130 Jermyn Street. When the ban was lifted is not known, but it is believed to have been applied very soon to only one stop, the pipes of which were up on the roof.

In the summer of 1927, the Plaza made the first British installation of Magnascope for the showing of *Chang*. This was a system for dramatically increasing the size of the picture for special sequences by the use of an enlarging lens on the projector and adjustable masking to open up the screen.

When Paramount took over the smaller Carlton Haymarket, that was used for extended runs of the company's more prestigious pictures and the Plaza played the other releases, usually with weekly changes, cultivating a regular audience.

It had no difficulty remaining one of the pre-eminent West End houses and it stayed open throughout the war. It entered the wide-screen era of the early Fifties not with CinemaScope but with Paramount's own VistaVision system for which an enlarged screen was installed to present *White Christmas*, the initial film in the new process, from 4 November 1954.

☐ Below and lower right, PLAZA in 1926. Upper right, foyer for dress circle in 1967, showing amazingly little change in 40 years.

□ **More views of the PLAZA in 1926.**

An even bigger screen, filling the entire width of the proscenium arch, made its debut on 16 June 1955 with *Strategic Air Command* when a double-frame horizontal system of projection was introduced. The screen was now 43ft. wide, masked to a height of 22ft. in the centre and 23ft. 10ins. at the edges, with a ratio of approximately 1.85 to 1. The much larger frame area that was projected (the same as on the original negative) ensured a much brighter, sharper image without visible grain. The film speed was doubled to project the normal 24 images per second. With the eventual abandonment of VistaVision, a Cinema-Scope-shape screen was introduced in the Sixties.

The Plaza's auditorium survived without alteration until 1967. By then its glory was faded but still apparent. The carpet in the main entrance hall or grand foyer was becoming threadbare. But one was still imbued with a sense of awe on a visit to the Plaza by the impression of space from lofty ceilings and tall doors and by the classical grandeur. The original architects (now Verity and Beverley) were retained to reconstruct the interior as two modern cinemas. The Plaza closed after a short run of a routine Paramount film *Gunn* on 27 September 1967.

What followed was the most expensive conversion that has been undertaken in a British cinema: the total cost (including fees and equipment) came to around £630,000. The partners in charge were Michael H. Hitchman and Sir Anthony Denny. Planning had begun on 25 May 1967 and work actually started the day after closure on a 38-week day-and-night basis, being completed on 17 June 1968. The Wurlitzer was removed to a private house after a final concert attended by 300 organ enthusiasts. Complaints over the noise of demolition and reconstruction resulted in one family living nearby being sent on holiday and another local inhabitant being moved to a hotel.

A 820-seat upper cinema was created using the rear section of the original balcony and building a new floor straight outwards from the original crossover to the rear wall of the former stage with a screen set up roughly where the fly tower had been. The former stalls area became a lower cinema seating 972. Its projection room was placed in the former Royal Circle and abstract panels were designed for the front side walls by Robyn Denny.

It was in this form that the building re-opened as the Paramount (downstairs) and the Plaza (upstairs), billed as "The Cinema with the Cinema Upstairs", on 27

July 1968. When Paramount combined with Universal to form Cinema International Corporation to release their joint output in Britain, the Plaza was re-named the Universal from 25 May 1972 to reflect the new partnership and the arrival of Universal pictures at the twin cinema. Paramount's Canadian cinema circuit, Famous Players, briefly became involved in running the cinemas and its tree logo appeared in advertising for a while.

Old names linger and everyone persisted in referring to the place as simply the Plaza. And so the cinemas became the Plaza 1 (downstairs) and Plaza 2 (upstairs) from 15 May 1975 when both played *The Godfather Part 2*.

It soon became apparent that the cinemas were too large for many films and so Plaza 1 closed in September 1977 to be tripled. The upstairs screen became the new Plaza 1. Downstairs, the front section became the 378-seat Plaza 2 which opened on 6 October 1977, served by the projection box already established in what was once the Royal Circle. The rear section was divided into two new cinemas with new projection boxes. Plaza 3 made its bow on Boxing Day 1977 with 163 seats while The Picture Palace at Plaza 4 opened on 28 January 1978 with 181 seats and a short-lived revival policy, after

□ **PLAZA in March 1991** *(ph: Allen Eyles).*

□ **After the 1977 twinning. Top, PARAMOUNT. Lower two, new PLAZA – note transparent curtains.** *(All three courtesy of* **The Architects' Journal**, *ph: Sam Lambert.)*

which it became simply Plaza 4.

And so half the 1967/8 conversion survives in the agreeably spacious Plaza 1. Plaza 2 retains decorative flourishes on the side walls and has a lofty ceiling while Plazas 3 and 4 are more nondescript.

In March 1983, the entrance moved from the corner of the site to one of the former shops on the Lower Regent Street side. The corner itself became an ice-cream parlour, serving patrons inside and passers by on the outside. A smaller advertising panel was placed above the corner, revealing much of the frontage that had been concealed by a much bigger panel since 1977, and an attractive new black terrazzo marble canopy was installed.

Like the Empire, the Plaza is now operated by UCI, the successor to CIC, and it shares the latest releases of Paramount and Universal through United International Pictures.

12 January 1927
Astoria
157 Charing Cross Road/ Sutton Row

This was an elaborate conversion of the Crosse & Blackwell pickle factory for which the architect was Edward A. Stone and the clients a company headed by E. E. Lyons and H. T. Underwood in association with Arthur Segal. The Astoria opened with *Triumph of the Rat,* had 1,650 seats, and was designed in Pompeiian style. A Compton organ was installed. Unusually, projection was from beneath the circle.

It was from designing this Astoria that Edward A. Stone went on to be the architect for the Astorias at Brixton, Old Kent Road, Streatham and Finsbury Park, working for Arthur Segal. They bore certain similarities of detail to the Charing Cross Road theatre, e.g. the exterior signs. Stone also designed a different set of Astorias for E. E. Lyons in a plainer manner at Brighton, Folkestone, etc.

This Astoria became part of the General Theatres Corporation circuit when that was formed in March 1928, and passed under Gaumont control with the rest of GTC two months later.

By the late Thirties the Astoria had declined to becoming a weekly change theatre, screening concurrently with the Metropole or New Victoria at Victoria. Closed with all other cinemas at the outbreak of war, it re-opened on 10 December 1939, closed during the height of the Blitz (from mid-September to 4 November 1940 except for a brief re-opening in October), then stayed open.

By the end of 1948 it was regularly playing a pre-release of the ABC circuit programme each week before it started its three-leg run through the London suburbs. The Tivoli soon became its partner, showing an identical programme.

Then, from 6 December 1956, the Astoria was returned to first-run programming with *Hollywood or Bust* as one of five Rank West End houses on premiere presentations. It was modernised with curtaining over of the side grilles and proscenium arch. It then became a road-show house with a new curved screen for extended runs of such big films as *Around the World in 80 Days* (from 2 July 1957), *Solomon and Sheba* (from March 1960), and *The Alamo* (from 27 October 1960). Seating was now 1,357.

For the world premiere of *The Fall of the Roman Empire* on 24 March 1964, the cinema was redecorated to accent the classical motifs in the auditorium (freize, columns, ceiling) with the circle lounge covered in a wallpaper of classical design and the main foyer given extensive Roman trimmings. In 1965, films such as *Those Magnificent Men in Their Flying Machines* and *The Agony and the Ecstasy* opened on the Astoria's huge 70mm screen for lengthy runs.

The cinema closed on 2 October 1968 to enable the interior to be gutted and a more intimate auditorium in a plain, modern style to be created with 1,121 seats. Re-opening took place on 17 December 1968 with *Chitty Chitty Bang Bang* but in time there proved to be an inadequate supply of even routine new films and a switch to a revival poilicy produced poor results. Rank closed the Astoria on 28 February 1976, having disposed of it for conversion into a live theatre. This involved further interior reconstruction (the stalls were raised 5ft. to provide a clear view of the stage) but projection facilities were retained and a film was screened in advance of performances of the first live show, the musical *Elvis* which opened on 28 November 1977. The Astoria closed again in 1979 to re-open on 15 June 1982 in a short-lived theatre-restaurant venture with a floor show called *Wild, Wild, Women*. A new stage show had a troubled run in 1983 and early in 1984 the Astoria was dark again. Since then it has become established as a live music venue, although the whole site is under threat of redevelopment as part of a reconstruction and enlargement of Tottenham Court Road Underground Station.

□ **ASTORIA. Right, exterior in 1948. Below, auditorium in 1927** (*right, from BFI Stills, Posters and Designs collection*).

26 March 1928
Carlton
Classic 1 2 & 3 Haymarket
Cannon 1 2 & 3 Haymarket
62/5 Haymarket

The Carlton was designed for use either as a cinema or as a live theatre. Paramount were closely involved in its construction and envisaged it potentially as a smaller sister cinema to the Plaza. It had the same architect—Frank Verity, working with Sam Beverley—and the shape and arrangement of the auditoriums, especially viewed from the stage, were remarkably similar after discounting the difference in size. The projection boxes were identically placed, protruding into the back row of the upper circle; the auditorium light fittings and the arrangement of the ceiling were the same in both cinemas; each had small royal circles at ground level, directly accessible from the foyer.

Yet the Carlton also had very extensive stage facilities and two boxes on the side walls. The stage was 60ft. wide (the proscenium opening only 42ft.), 45ft. deep, and 72ft. high (with its fly tower). There were fourteen dressing rooms.

The cinema trade expected the Carlton to open with a film but instead it made its debut on 27 April 1927 with a stage production, *Lady Luck*. It seated 1,159. Paramount first used the Carlton from 26 March 1928 for the four-month premiere

☐ **CARLTON in 1927, except top right from 1929** *(latter courtesy of* **The Architects' Journal**, *ph: Sydney W. Newbery).*

run of its silent epic, *Wings*. Then there were further live shows but in 1929 the Carlton was wired for sound and it became a cinema permanently from May onwards.

Paramount ran the Carlton for the next twenty-five years. While the company used its larger Plaza for weekly changes in the Thirties, the Carlton played the better or more sophisticated Paramount offerings on extended runs, usually with separate performances and bookable seats. Among the attractions of the early 1930s were the early Marx Brothers movies and such films as *The Love Parade*, *Love Me Tonight*, *Trouble in Paradise*, DeMille's *Cleopatra* and the Fredric March version of *Dr. Jekyll and Mr. Hyde*.

The Carlton closed after war was declared on 3 September 1939 along with all other cinemas, but its reopening was delayed until 29 December 1939 when Paramount had safely received a print of its cartoon feature *Gulliver's Travels* from America. It closed again in early October 1940, re-opening on 25 November of that year with *Northwest Mounted Police* when restricted opening hours meant only one showing daily at 2.30pm except for two shows on Saturday and Sunday at 2pm and 4.30pm. By late February 1941 the Carlton was managing three performances a day (12.10, 2.40 and 5.10) but the loss of evening performances explains why many other cinemas stayed dark at this time until the longer evenings and later blackout enabled them to at least stay open until 8.30pm. Eventually, regulations were relaxed and hours went back to normal.

In 1952, Jack Hylton was reported to be taking over the Carlton to return it to live theatre use, with films to end on 25 July. But Hylton's plans fell through. With a reduced output, Paramount no longer needed a second West End house besides the Plaza, and for some time had been booking many films from other American distributors to keep it going.

In 1954, 20th Century-Fox had a falling-out with Rank and arranged to take over the Carlton to showcase its own films. It became the third cinema (after the Odeons at Leicester Square and Marble Arch) to present films to the public in Fox's new CinemaScope process. With a "Miracle Mirror" screen and 26 stereophonic speakers spread behind the screen and around the auditorium, it made its debut under Fox management with the British premiere of *Beneath the Twelve Mile Reef* on 1 March 1954. The number of seats remained at 1,159.

For many years it prospered with the pick of Fox's output. In 1960, a fairly weak (but British quota) attraction *Let's Get Married* with Anthony Newley was supported by a special stage show which also featured the star. It was the last use made of the stage facilities.

During the Sixties, many top Fox attractions were siphoned off to the larger Rank cinemas in the West End after the rift was healed, but the Carlton fared well

☐ **As the CANNON HAYMARKET in March 1991** *(ph: Allen Eyles).*

enough. In 1969 Fox had plans drawn up to twin or triple the auditorium. Nothing happened but the Carlton was allowed to fall into a seedy state. *The Three Musketeers* enjoyed an exclusive first-run opening here in 1974 and ran twenty weeks but it was an exception with an increasing number of revivals keeping the doors open.

In 1977 Fox had new conversion plans drawn up but then decided to withdraw from exhibition in Britain. The Carlton was closed on 20 August 1977 following the run of *The Prince and the Pauper*. A campaign was launched to return the building to live theatre use but the Department of the Environment declined to list it.

The substantial stage end of the building was sold off and a small office block (Samuel House) erected there with an entrance on St. Alban's Street. Classic took over the rest of the building, converting it into a triple cinema which opened on Thursday 11 January 1979, with Classic 1 seating 491 upstairs (an adaptation of the old balcony with a new screen erected in front) and Classic 2 and 3 (201 and 222 seats) established downstairs.

The elegant Adam-style foyer has been most attractively maintained and visitors to Classic 1 can still obtain some sense of the old Carlton's interior from the little-altered side walls and ceiling, and the original light fittings. Some imagination and skill has been used to create a decorative pelmet for the screen curtain that blends in with the surroundings.

At 3am on Thursday 25 July 1985, fire broke out on one side of the foyer causing an estimated £750,000 of damage. It was treated by the police as a case of arson. Screens 1 and 2 were able to re-open on Friday 9 August, but restoration of screen 3 and one side of the foyer took longer, with that screen re-opening on 20 September.

On Friday 6 December 1985, the cinema was re-named Cannon along with all the other Classics.

26 April 1928
Tussaud's Cinema
Marylebone Road, Baker Street

Replacing the original makeshift cinema, this was a 1,714 seat lavishly appointed place (architect: F. Edward Jones) in the new Madame Tussaud's building. It opened with *Helen of Troy* and had a model F Wurlitzer. The organist was Edward O'Henry who regularly broadcast from the cinema on the old 2LO London radio station. There was also an orchestra or dance band attached to the cinema that performed at a series of Sunday afternoon celebrity concerts featuring at least two guest artists; the orchestra made numerous recordings in the Thirties.

The head of Associated British Cinemas, John Maxwell, became chairman of the owning company in February 1929 and the cinema was booked by ABC though not regarded as part of the circuit. Changes were weekly.

It was destroyed by German bombs on the night of 9/10 September 1940. The ruins were inspected by the King and Queen on the 20th. This corner of the Tussaud's building subsequently became the home of the Planetarium.

☐ **TUSSAUD'S CINEMA. Left, in 1928 with cinema entrance under nearest canopy in exterior shot** *(all three courtesy of Madame Tussaud's)*. **Below, after bomb damage in September 1940 (note modification to proscenium arch).**

8 November 1928
Empire
Leicester Square

In August 1925, the same year that it took over the Tivoli, Jury-Metro-Goldwyn (the British branch of Metro-Goldwyn, later Metro-Goldwyn-Mayer) announced its acquisition of the Empire music hall as the site for a new super cinema. The old Empire had moved in quickly after Lumière's Cinématographe had made its sensational debut on 20 February 1896 at the Polytechnic and it was transferred to Leicester Square on 9 March where it ran for eighteen months as a twenty-minute star attraction on the bill. Films continued to be featured at the old Empire (which was featured itself in Chaplin's *Limelight*). The King came to see footage of the Messina earthquake in January 1909; it was noted for its films of sporting events in 1912; seasons of features, such as D. W. Griffith's *Way Down East*, were shown in the early Twenties between musical shows. But the Empire closed on 22 January 1927 and was demolished. Property in Leicester Place and Lisle Street had been acquired to provide an enlarged site for a new cinema, on which British and American architects collaborated.

The eminent American cinema architect Thomas W. Lamb was undoubtedly the dominant figure in the new Empire's design, with the Frank Matcham practice, represented by F. G. M. Chancellor (Matcham had died in 1920), evidently being local consultants and supervisors. Certainly, the main facade was basically a copy of Lamb's design for the Albee Theatre in Cincinnati (opened 1927) while the tearoom under the circle (and, to some extent, the grand lobby) echoed Lamb's 1919 design for the Capitol Theatre in New York City.

The front of the cinema used a Venetian-arched motif backed by windows above ground level. In American fashion, the paybox was open to the street. The patron passed through one set of doors into the lobby, then through another set of doors into the grand foyer. Here the walls were panelled in dark walnut and mirrors between Corinthian pilasters while a huge glass chandelier hung from the ornate ceiling. The floor was carpeted (it wore out and had to be replaced in 1934 with a new handmade Axminster, weighing a ton and of similar if not identical design) and it led to a wide flight of centrally-placed steps down to the stalls foyer (and a foyer lounge to the left) and two flights of steps (carpeted marble) on each side rising to the landing and the large oblong tea-room beyond (in the void below the circle).

The auditorium was the biggest ever seen in the West End. Precise seating figures are hard to determine (the plans called for 3,344 seats) but 3,226 was the figure given out in the mid-Thirties, reducing to 3,100 in the early Forties. The huge circle extended over most of the stalls and had over 40% of the seats. The front edge of the circle was high above the stalls to allow a view of the screen from the back downstairs, and there was a large dome, lit by concealed lighting around the rim, set into the underside of the balcony to help suggest a real ceiling to stalls patrons. The decor was in High Renaissance style with a dado of walnut panelling and Corinthian pilasters flanking the arch, echoing the design of the grand foyer. There was huge dome in the main ceiling with its rim cut away at the rear to make way for the projection ports. A four-manual 20-rank Wurlitzer organ was installed and the stage was fully equipped for theatrical performances with rising platforms for the orchestra and organ console in the pit. The auditorium was set at right angles to the entrance with the stage end on Leicester Place and a side wall along Lisle Street.

The opening night attraction was Metro-Goldwyn-Mayer's silent *Trelawney of the Wells* supported by several newsreels and a talking interview with British stars at Elstree, plus selections from *Showboat* on the organ. The Empire charged 1s. 3d. for any seat from noon to 1pm, 1s. 6d. to 2s 4d. for seats between 1pm and 5.30pm, and 2s. 4d. to 3s. 6d. after that.

For the first week of *The Broadway Melody* (11-18 May 1929), the Empire sold tickets to 82,849 patrons – this remained the biggest week in its history (and undoubtedly the biggest week of any West End cinema ever). *Broadway Melody* ran nine weeks in all. (Details of all the films shown at the Empire, with their weekly admission totals, appeared in a special issue of the magazine *Picture House*, No. 13, Summer 1989.)

In 1937, the new basement cinema next door to the Empire was acquired by MGM, named the Ritz, and used to take over films from the Empire.

In December 1939, MGM's British-made *The Citadel* opened as the Christmas attraction and was a huge draw with wartime audiences during the respite of the "Phoney War". On Tuesday 27 December, the Empire achieved its biggest-ever daily attendance with 14,388 tickets sold. This film ran here for eight weeks.

Gone with the Wind was another

☐ **EMPIRE THEATRE Leicester Square. Facing page, exterior in 1928 and 1953 (in latter, note Ritz showing *Julius Caesar* at left and Monseigneur News Theatre in distance at right); and interior in 1961. Below, the Grand Foyer in 1928 with special wreaths for opening.**

☐ **Two views of the EMPIRE THEATRE's auditorium in 1928.**

tremendous attraction but its length prevented it from achieving record attendance figures. It opened concurrently at the Empire, Ritz and the Palace Theatre, staying for twelve weeks at the Empire.

With its excellent location and an outstanding succession of films, the Empire had good cause to label itself "The Showplace of the Nation" in the manner of the Radio City Music Hall. In August 1949, it was decided to enhance the Empire's appeal by making alterations (without closing the cinema) so that it could present stage shows in support of the feature like Radio City, bringing over one of that theatre's producers, Nat Karson, to put them on.

These shows started on Boxing Day 1949 in support of *The Forsyte Saga*. They featured the Empire Girls, the Empire Ballet, the Empire Singers and the Empire Concert Orchestra (conductor: George Melachrino) with variety acts that changed with each new show and included Max Wall and Monsewer Eddie Gray as early star attractions. An orchestra lift already existed from 1928 capable of bringing the orchestra up from the pit to stage level and down again. A back stage lift was installed that could raise an area 38ft. × 7ft. up in the air to a height of 6ft. 6ins. in 30 seconds. A compound unit was created for the front half of the stage, consisting of three independent units side by side across the stage which could be kept at stage level, lowered or raised to 6ft. 6ins. Perhaps the most spectacular feature of the shows was the "band car" or portable orchestra unit with its thirty-two instrumentalists which weighed five tons in all. Trackless and unguided, the band car worked from batteries at the touch of a push button by the orchestra leader. At the start of each show, it moved smoothly

forward from the back stage to the raised orchestra lift and descended. At the end, it rose and moved back onto the stage to join the other performers. There were four complete stage shows daily (except Sunday), taking less than an hour. A record number of 12,500 customers flocked to the Empire on Boxing Day 1949.

The stage show was intended to be changed for each new film presentation, but to be economic it had to last at least four weeks. *Annie Get Your Gun* ran for two months but too many other films

didn't have the same appeal, and it became necessary to retain the same stage show for two different pictures with the risk of deterring patrons who had already seen the first film from coming back when the supporting stage show was the same. Each show cost more than most West End productions to put on; cinema audiences began declining; and on 1 March 1952 the final stage presentation took place.

The Empire moved into the wide screen era with the installation of a new screen— 53ft. wide by 27ft.— which was masked down for its debut on 22 May 1953 to 40ft.

☐ **Part of the EMPIRE's frontage in 1954** (*from BFI Stills, Posters and Designs collection*).

by 23ft., its full width being reserved for presentations in CinemaScope (the first of which was *Knights of the Round Table* which opened on 12 May 1954 for a five-week run and had Perspecta stereophonic sound). The new screen was curved to a depth of 3ft. in the centre and tilted backwards 12 degrees from the vertical to reduce the keystone effect from the 28-degree projection rake.

Despite its popularity, the Empire was poor acoustically and its sightlines not that good. In 1954 the circle was closed so that new steppings could be laid down behind the front two rows and the crossover. The steppings were widened by 6ins. to 3ft. to provide more leg room and also raised to ensure a better view of the new wide screen. New seats were installed that were slightly wider than the old.

The Empire was still opening at 10am in the morning and films like *Guys and Dolls* and *High Society* ran for many weeks. But with 2,778 seats, it was clearly too large for most of the time and before 1960 it had been decided to construct a smaller cinema in its place.

However, the Empire was first to show the new *Ben-Hur*. For this, a new projection room was built in the centre of the stalls, resulting in the loss of half the stalls seating; and many side seats with poor views of the screen were removed. The projection throw was now only 78ft. and the seating capacity was reduced to 1,723. A new screen was installed, slightly wider than the proscenium arch and masked to a picture width of 52ft. *Ben-Hur* opened on 16 December 1959 and concluded its run at the Empire on Sunday 28 May 1961, transferring the next day to the Royalty.

The old Empire was completely gutted. A new Empire was built within the shell and opened in 1962.

29 November 1928
Regal
Odeon Marble Arch
Marble Arch/Edgware Road

The Regal was the first of a circuit that was built for A. E. Abrahams and his son David A. Abrahams (other Regals followed at West Norwood, Uxbridge and Edmonton). It occupied an imposing site at the western extremity of Oxford Street and the West End. The architect was Clifford Aish and it took seventeen months to construct.

There was a dignified, 110ft. high facade in Portland stone that was dramatically floodlit at night. There were three different entrances with canopies projecting, the main one being on the corner where Edgware Road began. For the auditorium, a Roman motif was adopted because on the site had once stood a Roman encampment to guard the strategic crossing of Watling Street (Edgware Road) and the Via Trinobantina (Oxford Street). Over forty different artists submitted decorative schemes for the interior and these were displayed at the Scala Theatre where the votes of nearly 500 visitors are said to have determined the choice of Charles Muggeridge as decorator. Many different kinds of cinema seating were also displayed and tested for comfort, the winner being installed at the Regal. The organ was specially designed by two experts and made by Christie's in England. It was the largest cinema organ in Europe and included a carillon, which was used for the signature tune of the regular broadcasts and which explained the legend "Hear the bells of Marble Arch" on the back of tickets.

The decorative scheme owed much to the "atmospheric" or landscape interiors that had been built in the United States to give audiences the impression of being seated outdoors. Here the suggestion was

of a Roman temple with glades of trees and garlands of creepers being visible behind a colonnade on the side walls, while through a massive pergola across the ceiling, covered in golden creeper, could be seen an imitation sky with twinkling stars and moving cloud patterns. The trees and foliage were fashioned in full or bas-relief to create a sense of depth.

The predominant colours used were those of autumn foliage—brown, red and gold. The seats were upholstered in panne velvet with a leaf design. A pattern of acanthus leaves ornamented the proscenium opening. Even the carpet advanced the scheme with a tile pattern on which scattered leaves were represented. Roman emblems such as masks and tripods were dotted around the auditorium while the gentle murmur of the two fountains at the base of the proscenium arch added to the woodland atmosphere (and, doubtless, the queues at the toilets). A gold-coloured curtain completed the scheme. There was no direct lighting anywhere.

A fully-equipped stage was provided. The owners had allowed for "every conceivable change or development in popular entertainment" and anything from intimate revue to grand opera was possible. The Regal made full allowance for the continued accompaniment of silent films with an orchestra pit and a lift which could raise the musicians to the level of the stage. However, the most up-to-date sound equipment was also installed. Two screens were provided and the speakers were set on lifts on the stage so that they could drop out of sight and the screen at the back used for silent pictures. There was a restaurant on the fourth floor (reached by stairs or either of two lifts) with a commanding view of Hyde Park.

Before opening, the Regal was leased to Arthur Gilbert's Hyde Park Cinemas Ltd., associated with his Suburban Super

□ **The REGAL Marble Arch in 1928.**

Cinemas Ltd. which already leased three picture houses from Abrahams. The first presentation at the 2,400-seat Regal was the Al Jolson talkie *The Singing Fool*, plus shorts and, live on stage, the June dancers. The Regal gave its first public audience on Thursday 29 November 1928 at 2pm.

In June 1929 the Regal was used for a late night press and trade show of the British talkie *Blackmail*, made by John Maxwell's British International Pictures. Soon after, Maxwell took over Hyde Park Cinemas in order to acquire the Regal for his ABC circuit. It became the shop window for BIP productions from 28 September 1929.

The Regal remained ABC's biggest West End house in the 1930s, although the circuit added first the Alhambra in 1929, then the London Pavilion circa 1932 and finally the Rialto in 1934 to provide a more central outlet for its B.I.P. productions. Many Warner Bros. pictures premiered here until the Warner Theatre opened in Leicester Square. After war broke out, ABC's Elstree Studios was requisitioned and the supply of major British films dried up, while attendances suffered generally. It had never been a great success but now the Regal was in severe difficulties and steadily losing around £1,000 per week. In January 1942, ABC had six years left on the lease under which it paid a weekly rent of £650 to Abrahams, who wanted £30,000 to tear up the deal. The Hyams brothers and others were keen to turn it into a music hall. This may well have prompted ABC to persevere with the Regal and try out a revival of cine-variety, a policy introduced with Jack Payne and Orchestra and singer Inga Andersen in support of the Fred Astaire and Rita Hayworth screen musical *You'll Never Get Rich* from 19 January 1942. The Regal relied on Columbia for most of its Hollywood films. However, it remained such a problem to run that ABC finally give up the theatre early in January 1945, following the run of *Janie*. Odeon negotiated to buy it for £250,000 and had just finished refurbishment when one of the last V bombs of the war struck.

The cinema was not able to re-open until 9 September 1945 when *A Bell for Adano* moved over from the Leicester Square Theatre. Renamed Odeon, it made weekly changes until it had the world premiere run of the British spectacular *Caesar and Cleopatra* which began on 13 December 1945 and lasted until 27 July 1946. Some more weekly programme changes ensued but the Odeon settled into premiere runs later in the year, notable titles including *Oliver Twist* in 1948 and *The Lavender Hill Mob* in 1951. In 1949, it was chosen to host the Royal Film Performance because King George was in such bad health that he needed the Odeon's lift to enable him to reach the circle. Some improvements were made to tidy up the remaining war damage before the Royals viewed The *Forsyte Saga* on the evening

□ **Two views of the REGAL Marble Arch's auditorium in 1928, lower showing Christie organ in raised position *(top from BFI Stills, Posters and Designs collection)*. See also picture facing title page.**

of 17 November, preceded by a stage show *Cinderella Meets the Stars* which featured such names as Margaret Lockwood, Gregory Peck, Anna Neagle, Rosalind Russell, Walter Pidgeon and Michael Wilding. (*The Forsyte Saga* opened to the public some weeks later at the Empire.)

The Odeon was the second West End cinema to open a CinemaScope picture, *How to Marry a Millionaire*. 20th Century-Fox leased it for one year to

showcase some of its other CinemaScope films beginning on 8 April 1954 with *King of the Khyber Rifles*. It then returned to Odeon and continued to be a leading West End cinema for the next few years. There was an increasing tendency to play low-brow pictures here as it was felt that most customers were drawn from the working class areas up the Edgware Road and it was a bit remote for regular West End audiences.

By the early Sixties, the originally

year lease to a property company in 1987, then leased it back on a short term basis. Since then, Apollo Leisure have become the operators of the building which was 'listed' by the Department of the Environment in 1988. Despite the shortage of such large venues in London and the clear demand for its facilities, there has been a reprehensible proposal to squeeze more money out of the site by building a new hotel and office block in its place, including all the adjacent properties. Camden Council sensibly refused planning permission and the developers were intent on forcing a lengthy public inquiry until one of the partners, a building company, ran into financial difficulties. The theatre was put up for sale and the American Nederlander organisation was interested in acquiring the Dominion for major musical presentations but was apparently outbid by a British property company. In 1991, the future of the Dominion remains a matter of concern.

15 October 1930
New Victoria
(Apollo Victoria)
Wilton Road and Vauxhall Bridge Road, Victoria

The New Victoria is unquestionably one of the most innovative and striking cinemas ever built in this country. Both externally and internally, it represented a complete break with tradition. At a time when major new cinemas were belatedly adopting the American atmospheric idiom (as at the Finsbury Park Astoria) or following classical precepts (the Elephant and Castle Trocadero), the New Victoria took its inspiration from German developments.

Formerly occupied by houses with basements and vaults under the pavements and by a much smaller cinema, the Victoria Picture Palace, the site was a rectangular one, 100ft. wide with extensive parallel frontages of 167ft. on two important streets, Wilton Road and Vauxhall Bridge Road. It had been acquired at a heavy cost of £250,000 by Provincial Cinematograph Theatres, which proposed to spend a similar amount on constructing a cinema. For

some time the site remained unused behind hoardings, awaiting a scheme that would fit in enough seats to make a cinema viable. Then the head of PCT, Will Evans, accepted the ideas of E. Wamsley Lewis for the site: these were to put the stalls floor underground and to fit the entrances, foyer, offices and lavatories into the space above the stalls and beneath the rear of the circle. Lewis set about designing the New Victoria in collaboration with PCT's chief architect, W. E. Trent. By the time it was completed and ready to open in October 1930, PCT had become part of the Gaumont-British combine.

The two frontages were very severe in style, with horizontal bands contrasted with strong vertical lines over the two entrances. The walls were faced in slabs of cast Portland stone, except for the ground floor where there were cast slabs of grey granite. The words "Exit" and "Stage Door" were cast in stone, as was a tiny figure of Chaplin. Taxi-drivers were said to have nicknamed the place "Sing Sing" as it went up. Above each entrance, there were two vertical grilles in pierced stone alongside two upright columns faced in shiny black Swedish

☐ **The Wilton Road entrance to the NEW VICTORIA in 1930.**

☐ Top left, the mermaid finial to stairs leading to circle, with paybox behind. Top right, broader view of the foyer from the same angle, showing the rubber flooring, doors on Vauxhall Bridge Road side, central laylight, and stairs to circle with bas-relief figure on back wall. Above, enclosed area at rear of stalls with wave-pattern carpet and marine decorative features. Right, 1971 view of rear stalls showing elaborate treatment of the soffit (*courtesy of former GLC Historic Buildings Division*).

granite. Neon lighting was set in horizontal bands along each side with vertical bands over the entrances – the 6,000 feet of neon tubes made it the largest installation of its kind. The Wilton Road side was enhanced by two bas-relief panels, sculptured in a French material called Lap by Newbury A. Trent. These were placed each side of the entrance, above exit doors and windows, and showed a mixture of ancients and moderns watching a film from an amphitheatre.

There was a spacious and striking entrance hall with rubber flooring and a ceiling dominated by a stepped-up central rectangular recess with a laylight in the ceiling. On one side of the entrance hall were two payboxes and stairs up to the rear circle with mermaid finials to the balustrades. At the head of the first set of stairs was another large panel de-

signed by Newbury A. Trent, featuring a woman, who represents the spirit of cinema, surrounded by spiralling strips of film. Other stairs, on the same side of the entrance hall, led down to the stalls while the front circle was quickly reached through doors on the other side. This area also accommodated a small cafe.

The auditorium was unique. "Imagine a fairy cavern under the sea, or a mermaid's dream of Heaven; something one has never seen or thought of before; huge submarine flowers against the walls that branch up and out and throw mysterious light towards the realms above, and glassy illuminated stalactites hanging from the ceiling; and a proscenium like a slender host of silver trees, and silvered organ pipes that shoot up to the roof; while over the whole the lights change from deep-sea green to the colours of the dawn, and from these to the warm comfort of sunlight." Thus ran the

description in *Gaumont-British News*, the company's house journal (October 1930).

W. E. Trent described it similarly in *The Bioscope* (15 October 1930): "The idea of the interior decorative scheme is a fairy palace under the sea – a place of one's dreams, fantastic, mystical, unlike any place of one's waking experience, built in unusual form, lighted by mysterious and beautiful lights. . . to produce in the spectator the proper frame of mind for relaxation." The marine theme was reinforced by various decorative features above doorways and around light fittings – mermaids, fish, shells – while a green carpet with a wavy design was used instead of the regular GaumontBritish design (red with laurel wreaths and the company logo). The seats were covered in green, blue and grey material patterned to evoke sea waves. The side walls had columns formed of a series of plaster shells with

64

□ **Two views of the NEW VICTORIA's auditorium in 1930, showing the original pendant light fittings (note also projection and spot boxes located in rim of dome in picture below).**

concealed lighting inside them. The under-balcony ceiling (or soffit) was decorated with a huge shelllike shape with concealed lighting.

The main ceiling was dominated by a large dome with a central light feature. Silver glass witch balls were hung from the valance surrounding the dome. Around the outside of the dome were eighteen glass stalactite fittings (more than half of them 12ft. long). Part of the dome could be slid open to admit daylight and fresh air, while the projection room was situated at the back of the dome, creating an exceptionally steep throw. Besides the projection room, the boiler house, heating and ventilating plant were placed on the roof of the building.

E. Wamsley Lewis has described the original colour scheme of the auditorium (*London Architect*, March 1972): "It was decided that while I wanted the plaster walls to be white, the public would think it bare, so we used the palest tints to give an over scaled mother of pearl effect, and I decided upon green basic lighting, with pink in some shell motifs, and white in the hanging glass stalactites, the green to be interchanged with light amber and certain blue lights but not amber." As Lewis declared, the scheme was strongly influenced by Hans Poelzig's Grosses Schauspielhaus in Berlin.

There was a Compton organ, but the pipes above the proscenium arch were dummies and the real pipes were behind in chambers with swell shutters. This location meant that the organ could only be heard in the balcony, not at all by the organist or patrons on the stalls floor. An amplifier was introduced in an attempt to rectify the problem.

According to the plans, the cinema seated 2,786 (1,076 in the balcony; (1,710 in the stalls), though a figure of 2,860 was later claimed. To fit in all these seats resulted in a huge balcony overhang but the vast expanse of soffit was strikingly decorated to avoid being too oppressive. At the rear of the stalls was a glazed partition, which looks like an afterthought, perhaps to eliminate noise. The side gangways of the stalls were actually under the pavements of Wilton Road and Vauxhall Bridge Road. One of the assistant architects, Keith P. Roberts, has put the total cost of the New Victoria at £125,000; E. Wamsley Lewis himself recalled it in 1972 as only £89,000.

The cinema opened with Warner Bros.' Hollywood production, *Old English*, starring George Arliss. Reginald Foort was at the organ, and there was a stage show, *Hoop-La*, imported from Paris and produced by Albert De Courville.

The invitational first night was a bit of a mess (as such occasions often were), although Arliss performed the opening ceremony and welcomed patrons via talking film on the screen. The souvenir programme was scrapped after the discovery that the agency providing it had

□ **The NEW VICTORIA circa 1945, showing war-time grime.**

innocently accepted an advertisement from British International Pictures, part of the empire of Gaumont-British's archrival, John Maxwell. The sound on *Old English* faded several times (two newspapers reported this and Gaumont-British retaliated by banning their critics from its press shows; they in turn declared a boycott on any mention of G-B's output). The opening stage show was widely criticised as being tedious and rated by one trade paper as poor value for the money allegedly spent. And Sidney Bernstein of Granada condemned the design concept of a mermaid's palace: "People don't want this sort of thing: they want architecture with marble columns, gilt and mirrors. This won't pay."

Shortly after the New Victoria had opened, a Dominions political conference took place in London and on November 5 it was arranged that the visiting prime ministers and the British Cabinet should watch a gala performance of extracts from British feature films plus shorts, with surplus seats being made available to the public.

The New Victoria was intended to take the premiere runs of Gaumont-British films. With its policy of a supporting stage show (which limited the feature to only three showings daily), it needed by one trade calculation to achieve ten capacity shows for every eighteen turnovers of audience to clear its overhead. Although *Old English* played longer as the opening attraction, the New Victoria's huge size and location meant that normally it could only keep films for a week, so ones that opened here like *On Approval* (with Tom Walls) later played a more central Gaumont cinema, like the Marble Arch Pavilion or New Gallery. The New Victoria also ran *Whoopee!* for a week

while it was in the middle of a long run at the Tivoli.

The expensive stage shows were dropped after a month and shorter ones substituted that allowed four showings a day of the main feature film, thereby saving costs and increasing potential revenue. Live variety and big bands continued to be a prominently advertised part of the programme into the mid-Thirties when it had been discontinued elsewhere. From the first December, 2,000 seats were offered at one shilling from opening at noon to 2pm (cut back to 1pm by 1933).

The New Victoria was handy for Buckingham Palace, and this was the reason it hosted a Royal Matinee performance of *The Good Companions* on the afternoon of 28 February 1933 in aid of the Personal Service League. King George V was a man of set ways and the show had to be timed to enable him to return to the Palace for his regular tea at five o'clock. This was the fore-runner of the Royal Film Performances which became an annual event after the war.

Later in the 1930s, programming at the New Victoria shifted to big-value double bills of films that had already played the West End. When war-time bombing became particularly intense at the end of September 1940 and cinema opening hours were curtailed, the New Victoria was forced to close. It re-opened on 25 May 1941 with a double bill that combined the first features from the Astoria and Dominion. It was during the war years that the eighteen stalactite light fittings around the ceiling were removed as a safety measure, never to be restored. (It is not so clear when the subsidiary canopies by the two entrances were taken away, or when the vertical grilles by each side of the main canopies, which were illuminated from within, were filled in.).

Later in the 1940s the New Victoria was paired up with the Dominion Tottenham Court Road and they became pre-release theatres for the Gaumont circuit, playing each programme for a week before it went around the London suburbs at prices between the West End and local cinemas. (This paralleled the use of the Metropole and Odeon Tottenham Court Road as pre-release halls for the Odeon circuit, and the use of the Astoria and Tivoli for the pre-release of ABC circuit programmes.) Most main features had played in the West End earlier but some weaker programmes and most supporting features given a Gaumont circuit release received their first British showings here and at the Dominion. Despite the steep throw, CinemaScope images looked fine at the New Victoria, although the wide screen was rather small compared to the original screen.

In the autumn of 1956, at a time when the Rank Organisation (owners of the Odeon and Gaumont circuits) decided to close a considerable number of marginal cinemas, it also reached the conclusion that the New Victoria was far too large for the number of attendances it was achieving, even though it was making an average annual profit of £20,000. Various conversion proposals were explored. The original idea was to retain an 800-seat cinema in the circle, use the stalls floor for a ballroom and redevelop the stage area for shops. Architects T. P. Bennett and Sons drew up plans in August 1957. In November of that year, consideration was given to retaining the stalls as a cinema and putting the ballroom overhead, but in the same month it was decided to drop the ballroom idea and Rank's estate agents were asked to investigate whether there would be any interest in a ground floor provision for a supermarket. The answer was not encouraging and, in view of the very high costs of inserting a new floor at ground level (because the stalls were much lower), the idea of subdividing the New Victoria was temporarily abandoned.

In 1958, the stage installation was overhauled and the dressing rooms re-instated to allow the New Victoria to be rented out for a live show, *Where the Rainbow Ends*, which opened on Boxing Day. Like the Dominion, the New Victoria was now available for occasional live use.

In October 1963, a preliminary scheme was drawn up by architects on Rank's instructions to show how the New Victoria could be split horizontally into two smaller cinemas, one using the stalls and the other the circle extended forwards on a gentler stepping. In both cases, new screens would have been placed in front of the old pros arch and the stage would have been freed for other uses. This and similar plans for large provincial Odeons were not carried out then. Although Rank did twin its Nottingham Odeon in 1965 and others later in the decade, the New Victoria was spared – perhaps because it was no longer owned by Rank following a sale-and-leaseback arrangement in 1964.

The New Victoria was more eclectic in its film programming in the Sixties. It never became a roadshow house, although it did play occasional two-week or longer pre-release runs of films like *Goldfinger* and *The Graduate* concurrent with key suburban cinemas. By this time, there was a modern back-lit readagraph perched on each canopy, announcing the current attraction – the days had long gone when each programme would be announced in neon-covered letters spread out in the tall frame below the main New Victoria signs.

Apparently, the early introduction of cable television to the Victoria area hit cinema attendances quite badly. As film attendances declined, the New Victoria's stage facilities were brought into fuller use, and there were many one night stands, regular seasons of the Royal Festival Ballet from 1964 to 1975, and many shows featuring the Black and White Minstrels. These were, of course, disruptive to regular attendance by cinemagoers and, as far as films were concerned, the New Victoria seemed to slide down-market, playing many sex and horror programmes that were probably more economical to book.

In 1972, the New Victoria became one of the first cinemas (along with the Granada Tooting) to be 'listed' for its architectural significance. In 1973, probably as an outcome of this, the auditorium was re-wired and repainted in warm, red colours (totally inappropriate, of course, to its underwater theme). Seating by this time was 2,574. It closed as a cinema rather suddenly on 1 November 1975, the last films being a double bill of *Legend of the Werewolf* and *Vampire Circus*. Rank had arranged to sub-let it to impresario Danny O'Donovan's Videpalm company from 10 November for live shows. These did not seem to work, and there was considerable concern over the future of the building, despite its being listed.

Apollo Leisure acquired Rank's lease for 21 years from 2 May 1980. Designer Michael Sassoon was commissioned to give some "razzamatazz" to the building. He was responsible for the red glitter paintwork and the Tivoli chandelier hung in the centre of the foyer, while the star dressing rooms were much improved to welcome the celebrity acts booked to appear there. It re-opened as the Apollo Victoria on Monday 15 September with a week of Shirley Bassey in concert (all shows were fully sold out in advance), followed by Cliff Richard (whose three-week appearance was also fully booked beforehand), Gladys Knight and the Pips, Elkie Brooks, and others. Then came two musical revivals, *The Sound of Music* with Petula Clark and *Camelot* with Richard Harris. For *The Sound of Music* the proscenium arch was dressed up to look like the Alps. *Fiddler on the Roof* was another musical hit revived here, with Topol starring. Apollo Leisure were sufficiently encouraged to purchase the freehold from the landlords and own the building outright from the end of 1982.

Then in 1984, Andrew Lloyd-Webber's musical extravaganza *Starlight Express* opened and it has been there ever since. We must be thankful that a hit show has given the New Victoria a new lease of life, and that listing of the building was upgraded to grade II* in mid-1985. But, unfortunately, the auditorium can hardly be seen for the multi-tiered set with its mass of steel-work supporting video screens, model railway tracks and ramps for the roller-skating cast that extend all around the stalls floor and across the front of the circle creating a total "stage" a quarter of a mile long. At least one of the decorative features, a dolphin above the rear stalls entrance, has disappeared.

There are indications that the interior will be restored to some of its former glory if ever the show closes. It would be nice if a complete grant-aided restoration could be carried out to the kind of standard seen in the United States at the Fox Detroit and many, many other former movie palaces put to the same kind of use as the New Victoria.

In 1989, the stonework outside was cleaned on both frontages and the New Victoria signs high up removed, which leaves the space above the canopies looking much too bare (especially as the black columns are now only black to half their height). For the rest of each facade, the reintroduction of horizontal neon (for which the slots remain) would be a great enhancement and make the New Victoria, or Apollo Victoria as it must now be called, really eye-catching by night.

☐ **One of the decorative panels above exit doors on the Wilton Road frontage of the NEW VICTORIA in 1991. Note also vertical Exit sign in stone at left.** *(Ph: Allen Eyles.)*

19 December 1930
Leicester Square Theatre
RKO Leicester Square Theatre
Olympic
Leicester Square Theatre
Odeon West End
39-41 Leicester Square/
St. Martin's Street

It was Jack Buchanan who had the idea of putting up a theatre on the south-west side of Leicester Square. He and Walter Gibbons purchased the site in December 1928 and set about building the theatre for a quarter of a million pounds with Andrew Mather as their architect (he designed the Capitol for Gibbons earlier).

Buchanan planned to manage it rather than appear there himself and it was to be called the Buchanan Theatre. However, when hopes of acquiring properties at the rear of the site were dashed, this left insufficient space for a full stage and it was redesigned during construction for dual variety and cinema use. There were 1,760 seats on three levels and a Wurlitzer was installed.

United Artists toyed with making it their showcase theatre and opening Chaplin's *City Lights* there but chose the Dominion instead. It was Warner Bros. who provided the opening night film, *Viennese Nights*, which was supported by a stage show. In March 1931, the American RKO company took over on a three

☐ **LEICESTER SQUARE THEATRE. 1939 night exterior and 1946 daytime exterior. Auditorium in the 1930's and (below right) after 1968 reconstruction** (*latter courtesy of Rank Theatres*).

year lease from Walter Gibbons and re-opened it as the RKO Leicester Square Theatre in June after the interior had been redesigned by Edward Carrick and a revolving stage installed. It closed during August and some months later RKO passed it on to County Cinemas who had Alister MacDonald re-design the entrance. County re-opened it as the Olympic at the end of March 1932 with *In a Monastery Garden* but found the going so tough they closed it on 3 July. It reopened under its original name as a variety house the following month.

Jack Buchanan recovered control and leased it to United Artists to re-open on 27 September 1933 with Buchanan's own film *That's a Good Girl*. A stream of other United Artists releases played here, including another Buchanan picture, *Brewster's Millions*, in 1935.

The building closed again on 18 July 1937, supposedly for a redecoration scheme by Buchanan himself to be carried out, and seemed likely to re-open as a variety theatre. But Buchanan threw in with General Cinema Finance Corporation (J. Arthur Rank, C. M. Woolf) whose associated company, General Film Distributors, programmed and ran the theatre. It had become the first Rank West End cinema.

War damage put the theatre out of action from late October 1940 and destroyed the flat that Jack Buchanan had always had at the top of the building. Re-opening took place on 11 July 1941 with *The Flame of New Orleans*. In July 1946, Rank re-organised his interests and the cinema passed from GFD to Odeon.

With the right pictures, the cinema was in an excellent location to attract audiences, and over the years it has been second only to the Odeon across the square among Rank's West End houses. It closed for two months in 1955 (26 May to 27 July) for war damage to be fully repaired, a new canopy installed, the entrance hall remodelled, and the auditorium redecorated, preserving the original decorative plasterwork.

Total reconstruction occurred at the end of the run of *Carry On Doctor* on 3 April 1968. It cost £285,000 and the architects were Arnold Dick Associates with an interior design by Cassidy, Farrington and Dennys. The gallery was closed and the separate side entrance on St. Martin's Street bricked in. A new lightbox was installed above the canopy, much lower than the original neon lettering display area, and the theatre's name was moved down also.

The completely new auditorium seated 1,407—900 in the stalls, 507 in the circle. The walls were the natural white of plaster onto which spotlights at the back of the circle and on the circle front played changing colours. Concealed trough lighting all the way around the edge of the circle created an impression that it floated in space. Seating was in five colours—mauve, blue, green, orange and shocking pink. The stage end was rebuilt and the screen set 50ft. further back.

It was in this form that the Leicester Square Theatre re-opened with *Shalako* on 12 December 1968.

On Friday 22 July 1988, with the opening of a comedy called *The Couch Trip*, the cinema was renamed the Odeon West End and it continues as a large single screen cinema, usually with exclusive runs.

12 September 1933
Victoria Station News Theatre
Victoria Station Cartoon Cinema
Platform 19, Victoria Station/ Buckingham Palace Road

This was the first British news theatre to open in a station, and the auditorium ingeniously used wasted space above ground level. It was perched on columns 16ft. off the ground over a carriageway from Buckingham Palace Road for taxis and other vehicles, and underneath the existing roof of Victoria Station. Patrons had direct access to the News Theatre at ground level from Buckingham Palace Road as well as from the station by a common lobby. After purchasing tickets, it was necessary to climb a long staircase contained within a streamlined structure with a stepped frontage, strikingly carried out in the Modern Movement style and suggestive of a 1930s signal cabin or ocean-liner or locomotive. The barrel shaped, cavern-like single-floor auditorium had 235 seats. The walls and floor were specially insulated against noise and vibration from traffic passing underneath and from the station generally.

"Whilst waiting for your train, why not visit the News Theatre?", the station announcer would say, and its whereabouts were indicated by signs all over the station. This was an ideal location: people who had missed a train, were waiting for a delayed arrival, or wanted a rest or to treat the children, would be drawn in to see the programme of newsreels, serials and shorts. To the left of the screen was a clock giving the exact time, while to the right when it first opened a small screen showed the arrivals and departures for the next ten minutes. The projectionist was kept informed by telephone of any changes to pass on to patrons.

☐ **The streamlined entrance to the VICTORIA STATION NEWS THEATRE in 1933. The beginning of the auditorium at right angles with a supporting column is just visible at right.** *(From National Monuments Record.)*

The auditorium of the VICTORIA STATION NEWS THEATRE in 1933 with small screen for train announcements on right. *(From National Monuments Record.)*

The architect was Alister G. MacDonald, who had previously designed the Sphere News Theatre and who later created the Waterloo Station News Theatre, very similiar to the one at Victoria. The Victoria Station News Theatre was built for London News Theatres which became Capital and Provincial News Theatres.

During the height of the Blitz, the cinema closed, re-opening in late May 1941.

When newsreels ceased, this News Theatre became the Victoria Station Cartoon Cinema. Although business declined, it did well enough to be still operating in 1981, the very last of its kind in the country, and it was never switched to feature films. (A practical drawback to the introduction of longer programmes was that it had no public lavatories of its own.) The lease expired at the end of

☐ As the VICTORIA STATION CARTOON CINEMA in October 1977, the block of the auditorium behind old News Theatre display board, above roadway. *(Ph: Allen Eyles.)*

July 1981 and was renewed for one month. The Cartoon Cinema then closed on Thursday 27 August 1981 to make way for the construction of the Victoria Place shopping plaza overhead. The last show included a Movietone newsreel of the 1937 Coronation, specially arranged by the projectionist. The road that passed underneath the cinema is now the goods entrance for the shopping plaza and provides a means of public access to the station.

6 March 1934
Curzon
Curzon Street/ West Chapel Street

The Curzon was designed by Francis Lorne of Sir John Burnett, Tait and Lorne in a European style of stark simplicity. The low frontage was partly the result of fierce opposition to a cinema opening in the heart of Mayfair and it had to be less than 35ft. high. A plain brick exterior with a horizontal emphasis was arrived at, with a white stone canopy over the entrance intersected by a perpendicular projection which carried a neon sign spelling out the cinema's name in a lazy, flowing green neon scrawl. Programme advertising was originally very discreet, confined to the entrance area.

Inside, the 492-seat auditorium was devoid of decoration, with the walls and ceiling covered in flesh-tinted stippled plaster on which three different colours of lighting played from concealed positions inside the five curved sconces that crossed the ceiling, parallelling the curve of the proscenium arch. The seating, all on one floor, was upholstered deep blue and the doors painted scarlet. The three back rows consisted of club seats raised above the other seating and enclosed by a maple barrier. There was no stage but three steps in front of the tabs.

The Curzon's design was highly suitable for its function as an elite art house under the direction of the Marquis de Casa Maury, a decorative artist who had been impressed by the simplicity of some Parisian cinemas he had seen and demanded a similar treatment here. A starting price of 2s. 6d. (compared to 1s. 6d. at its rivals, the Academy and Cinema House) reflected its up-market ambitions.

The Curzon closed on 2 September 1939 for redecoration until 14 September. But the declaration of war on 3 September

☐ The CURZON, "the haunt of titled people and their butlers", in 1934.

□ The CURZON in 1934 (*from BFI Stills, Posters and Designs collection*).

20 August 1934

Eros News Theatre
Eros Cartoon Theatre
Classic Cartoon Theatre
Eros
7 Shaftesbury Avenue, Piccadilly Circus

The Eros News Theatre provided a clever instance of squeezing a cinema into a thoroughly inadequate space. The distinguished architect for the 203-seat newsreel theatre was Robert Atkinson. He had a tall, narrow space to contend with, and the result was a cinema entered at the screen end, with a small balcony reached at just below street level and the stalls entered by descending a staircase behind the screen. The projection box was placed over the balcony, throwing a upwards to reduce distortion. One curious result of the awkward site was that the projection room could only be entered from the adjacent building off a hallway leading to various offices.

□ EROS NEWS THEATRE, circa 1935. (*Exterior ph: John Maltby.*)

Wollenberg died during one of the performances – perhaps the happiest way for a film buff to go?) The film clocked up a further run at the Berkeley.

An associated distribution company— GCT, later Curzon Film Distributors— supplied many of its presentations including *The Diary of a Country Priest* and *The 400 Blows*. From time to time, the Curzon would play safe with commercial attractions like the Bardot *Heaven Fell That Night* but its overall policy was an adventurous one.

The original Curzon couldn't by itself provide an adequate return on the prime space it occupied, so it was closed on 28 August 1963 to make way for an office block incorporating a new Curzon which opened in 1966.

resulted in the cinema staying closed until much later when it was taken over by the Directorate of Army Cinematography for army screenings.

After the war it was acquired by H. H. Wingate's General Cinema Theatres and re-opened to the public on Thursday 14 February 1946 with *Love Eternal*. The Curzon came to have a reputation second only to the Academy as an art house. Hit films could clock up enormous runs, like *La Ronde* which played 2,424 performances from 27 April 1951 to 9 October 1952 and was seen by over half a million paying patrons. (Critic and co-editor of the *Penguin Film Review* H. H.

5 September 1934
London Pavilion
**Piccadilly Circus/
 Shaftesbury Avenue**

This landmark building's exterior dates from 1885. Films were first shown here in a season of film-only matinees in 1908 but it became the last West End music hall to include the bioscope in its regular shows, finally succumbing to its charm (and box-office appeal) in April 1911. The Pavilion later became a full-time cinema for short periods – Famous Players (Paramount) showed films like *The Covered Wagon* here in 1923/24 – and there were many films shown by arrangement with Charles Cochran from 1929 onwards, including *The Taming of the Shrew* with Fairbanks and Pickford, Ronald Colman in *Condemned*, and the lengthy run of *Hell's Angels* with pictures and sound on separate projectors (the old British Acoustic system). It was under ABC circuit control showing exclusively British pictures for a while until May 1932.

But its real life as a West End cinema began after it was closed on 7 April 1934 and underwent almost complete internal reconstruction to plans by F. G. M. Chancellor of the late Frank Matcham's practice for A. E. Abrahams with Cecil Masey representing United Artists, the new lessees. The awkwardly-shaped island site made planning difficult and the three levels of stalls, circle and upper circle were retained, despite some awkward sightlines from the rear stalls and up in the gods, so that an economic number of seats—1,209 in all—could be squeezed into the restricted space. The stalls seated 716 with 242 in the circle and 251 in the upper circle. The decor was somewhat plain but some idea of the original decorative scheme could be obtained from the underground stalls salon which was hardly touched.

The London Pavilion was re-opened on 5 September 1934 by United Artists, who had at long last settled on their West End showcase and who continued to operate it until closure in 1981. Only a temporary three-week closure at the height of the Blitz in late October 1941 seems to have interrupted its progress.

☐ **LONDON PAVILION in 1948.** *(From BFI Stills, Posters and Designs collection.)*

☐ **The EROS** *(photographed in December 1982 by John Edwards for the Museum of London).*

The fittings, such as the surviving entrance door, were of a high standard and the now disused cove lighting in the lofty ceiling had a dramatic effect. The cinema was operated by Capital and Provincial News Theatres (who later took over the Classic circuit). The company had already opened news theatres of similarly ingenious construction at Victoria and Waterloo (although those were high above ground).

With its superb location looking onto Piccadilly Circus and the statue of Eros, the cinema has always scooped up passing trade. After newsreels were abandoned, it continued as a cartoon theatre, eventually taking the Classic name, until 1976 when it switched to sex films on Thursday 29 April with *Love in a Women's Prison* plus *Sins within the Family* and reverted to the Eros name it had had for a long time previously.

The exterior of the Eros featured in the 1981 film *An American Werewolf in London*, although the auditorium was a studio set. The Eros finally closed with the Bo Derek film *Bolero* on 14 February 1985. The entrance and auditorium are now occupied by H. Samuel, the jewellers, and no sign of a cinema remains. The distinctive entrance doors and some other decorative features were saved for the Museum of London.

In the post-war years, all kinds of "floating" product would be booked into the hall, frequently in double-bills and usually lending itself to lurid publicity. From the mid-Fifties, a better class of picture often played here because UA had such a massive line-up of releases— from thick-ear adventures like *Vera Cruz* to "difficult" films like *The Miracle Worker*.

Over the years the Pavilion's exterior had become covered in a much-loved hodgepodge of neon signs and the original 1885 facade (by J. E. Saunders and R. J. Worley) could hardly be seen. In the late Seventies, the signs were taken down and the 'listed' frontage redecorated to reveal its forgotten splendour.

By this time United Artists were finding it hard to programme their cinema with profitable attractions and it closed on 26 April 1981 with a typically weak offering, *The Idolmaker*, that had overstayed its welcome. The final seating capacity was 1,004 (511 stalls; 241 dress circle: 252 upper circle).

Theatre managements were keen to turn the place into a live theatre but it was announced that the building would be split into a shopping mall with two smaller (each 500 seat) cinemas above.

But no-one seemed keen to take the cinemas at the price entailed, and the upper part of the building has become Madame Tussaud's wax museum for rock 'n' roll stars.

☐ **LONDON PAVILION. Top and centre, auditorium in 1981 just prior to closure** (*courtesy of the Museum of London, ph: John Edwards*). **Right, the recently refurbished exterior after closing with canopy and entrance advertising new films at other cinemas** (*ph: Keith Skone*).

1 November 1934
Monseigneur News Theatre
Jacey
Centa
Cinecenta 1 & 2
Cannon Piccadilly
215 Piccadilly

The basement Monseigneur restaurant was converted into a newsreel theatre in just twenty-two days under the direction of architect Cecil Masey. Changes were necessarily modest and the main decorative features of the restaurant were retained. The floor was left flat rather than sloped, and 284 seats were installed. Part of the old restaurant balcony was converted into the projection room; another part was retained as a café from which the screen could be watched. The original entrance at 215 Piccadilly was barely altered. The name Monseigneur was retained and used in a series of similar conversions to form the small circuit of West End news theatres at Strand, Trafalgar Square and Marble Arch (there were others outside London).

☐ **CANNON PICCADILLY in March 1991** *(ph: Allen Eyles).*

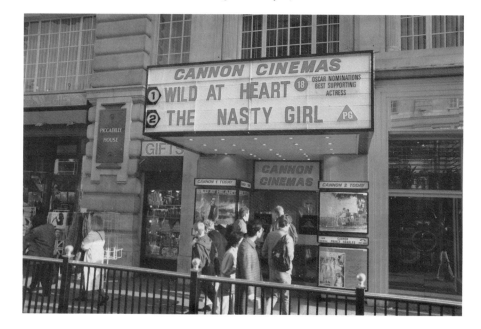

The first Monseigneur functioned as an air raid shelter during the war. In June 1960 the entire circuit was taken over by Jacey. From 9 July 1964, this cinema was turned over to features beginning with *London in the Raw*. Programming was varied but with the accent on sexy 'X' certificate films.

The expanding Cinecenta group acquired it from 1 May 1972 and renamed it the Centa. It was closed at the end of October 1979 to be twinned. The Star group took over Cinecenta in December 1979 and were in charge for its re-opening as the Cinecenta 1 & 2 on 7 February 1980 with the 3–D *What the Swedish Butler Saw* plus *Blue Fantasies* in the 118-seat number 1 screen and *Zombie Flesh Eaters* plus *Tool Box Murders* in the 124-seat number 2 screen. The old auditorium was split down the middle, creating two long cinemas with entry at the screen end.

Renamed the Cannon Piccadilly from Friday 6 December 1985, the cinemas continue in business mostly with films opened elsewhere with a leaning towards sexually explicit fare.

29 August 1935
Monseigneur News Theatre
Jacey in the Strand
284 Strand

Cecil Masey was again the architect for this second Monseigneur News Theatre which involved the conversion of part of the east wing of Shell-Mex House into a 269-seat auditorium reached by a narrow entrance from the Strand. The floor between the ground and first floors was knocked out and exits provided onto the colonnaded pavement along the side wall of the theatre around the edge of the inner courtyard.

The cinema opened with a single admission chage of one shilling for all seats. There were plans to present televised pictures at a time when it was thought most people would watch television in cinemas.

The Monseigneur weathered the years quite comfortably, emphasising cartoons when newsreels were phased out. It was part of the circuit when Jacey acquired it in June 1960 and it went on to become the first of the Jacey group of news theatres to go over to features. After a re-fit, it re-opened on 23 February 1961 as the Jacey in the Strand, initially attempting an up-market art house policy but soon settling down to sexploitation fare. When this policy no longer worked, revivals of horror classics and *Citizen Kane* were tried out during 1965, then came a series of mainstream big budget revivals like *West Side Story* and *Exodus*. It was one of these—*Lawrence of Arabia*—that closed the theatre following a week's run from 6 to 11 January 1966.

The entrance and auditorium was first converted into an arcade of stamp shops. Then, late in 1983, workmen converted the auditorium into offices with new windows onto the courtyard. The entrance area in 1991 is the Hebe hair salon.

☐ **As THE JACEY IN THE STRAND in 1961.**

☐ **Following modernisation, as THE JACEY IN THE STRAND in 1961.**

10 February 1936
Paramount
Odeon Tottenham Court Road
Tottenham Court Road/
Grafton Street

Even though Paramount had two West End theatres, the Plaza and Carlton, they erected a third, even larger one at the north end of Tottenham Court Road on the site formerly occupied by Shoolbreds Department Store. With 2,568 seats (1,676 in the stalls and 892 in the circle) it was the third largest West End cinema in seating capacity after the Empire and Dominion.

Frank Verity, with his partner Sam Beverley, was the architect for this, as he had been for the Plaza and Carlton, and for the provincial Paramounts. The theatre was built in five months for £108,000 (including £6,000 in fees and £12,500 of outfitting but excluding the cost of the site). The auditorium was set at right angles to the narrower entrance hall on the corner.

The Paramount operated a policy of double-bill programmes changed weekly (on Sundays). On all days but Sunday, a live show was included featuring the Compton (Reginald Foort was the first organist), the Paramount Orchestra, the Paramount Tiller Girls, and specially engaged variety acts. Programmes began at noon and until 4pm prices were 9d., 1/– and 1/6 rising to 1/–, 2/– and 2/6 after 4pm. A spacious café seating 130 was located over the corner entrance serving dainty teas and light refreshments. It was open to patrons and the general public from 10am to 10pm.

Films were shown in advance of their suburban release and this resulted in considerable uproar at the time of the Paramount's opening over the extension of the existing pre-release area at the expense of other cinemas like the Gaumont Camden Town.

According to Benny Green in a humorous recollection of the cinema (*London Daily News*, 11 April 1987), "In no time, the Paramount became a local institution. On Saturdays whole families would disappear inside its darkened interior, determined to see the bill through three times, and equipped for the enterprise with carrier bags bursting with supplies. Because the larger groups never managed to sit together, the food was aimed all over the place. People used to say that all a starving beggar had to do to stay alive was sit in the Paramount with his hand in the air, because it was only a matter of time before a cheese sandwich or a chicken leg landed there."

This Paramount was in a second batch of the company's theatres purchased by the Odeon circuit in July 1942 and taken over the following month. It was renamed Odeon in November 1946, by which time it regularly played, along with the Metropole Victoria, the Odeon circuit programmes for a pre-release week before they went out into the London suburbs.

□ **The spectacular look of the PARAMOUNT Tottenham Court Road by night in 1938, plus a 1936 daytime shot below.**

The first British installation of the new wide-screen CinemaScope process occurred here and it was demonstrated to exhibitors on 30 June 1953 on a 53ft. x 21ft. screen, curved 3ft. deep in the centre. However, the public didn't see CinemaScope here until much later.

In 1958, the Odeon was fitted up with a new giant-screen Cinerama-like process called Cinemiracle to present the first film in the process, *Windjammer*, on a separate performances extended run beginning in May. The huge 71ft. x 28½ft. screen extended beyond the proscenium arch into the auditorium and was said to be the largest in the country. Three projectors were installed in the specially-built projection room at the rear of the stalls. Over 700 seats were lost, reducing capacity to around 1,700. Unfortunately, Cinemiracle didn't last more than six months.

By 1960 the Odeon had reverted to weekly changes of circuit programmes, generally presenting the new Rank release with the New Victoria a week

□ **The circle lounge (above the entrance) and auditorium of the PARAMOUNT Tottenham Court Road in 1936.**

1936
Monseigneur News Theatre
Jacey Trafalgar Square
4 Grand Buildings

Part of the basement of Grand Buildings on the south-east corner of Trafalgar Square was Cecil Masey's next conversion job for the Monseigneur circuit. The resulting 300-seat cinema, entered through a former shop at ground level to the right of the arcade entrance, was well-positioned to catch the eye of tourists visiting Nelson's column. Jacey's take-over of the Monseigneur circuit led to it being called Jacey Cartoon Cinema from 1962 (newsreels had been discontinued).

It went over to feature films (usually of a sexy nature) from 18 June 1970, becoming simply the Jacey and beginning with *She Lost Her You Know What*. Such lurid titles prominently displayed on the otherwise dignified facade of Grand Buildings were a distasteful intrusion on the Square with its quite different character from Leicester Square. Briefly renamed the Jacey Trafalgar Cinema on Thursday 13 October 1977, and soon reverting to Jacey, the cinema closed abruptly on 23 July 1981 with the last showings of *Seduction* and *French Love*. It was the last Jacey cinema in the West End. The seats and equipment were subsequently installed at the Regal Cranleigh and the entrance turned into a gift shop. Since then the entire building has been demolished and rebuilt, copying the original facade.

□ **JACEY TRAFALGAR SQUARE, circa 1971** *(ph: Keith Skone)*.

before it began the rounds. However, its final programme was a CinemaScope picture booked onto the National circuit, *The Story on Page One*, and it closed on 5 March 1960 to be demolished. The temporary car park on the site (behind advertising hoardings) is still in use thirty years later! As Benny Green summed up: "I would like to say to the unknown rat who knocked the Paramount down that having taken such trouble to dig such a big hole, the best thing now would be for him to go and jump into it." The cinema's original name is commemorated in the adjacent Paramount Court block of flats which were also designed by Verity and Beverley and built a little later than the picture house.

7 March 1936
Studio Two
Studio 4
225 Oxford Street

Studio Two was a conversion of the basement Chinese restaurant (London's first) in Cinema House (see 1910) to plans of Leslie H. Kemp and F. E. Tasker for D. J. James. It was a considerable engineering feat to insert the steelwork for the new cinema without damaging the existing cinema (which was temporarily closed) or the three floors of offices above that.

Studio Two opened on 7 March simultaneously with the re-opening of Cinema House as Studio One. The new addition seated 370 and operated on a 'news and travel' policy. (News flashes could be read off a strip underneath the screen.) It was entered at the screen end, passing through a new, smaller cafeteria area, and the projection box was situated behind and below the screen of Studio One. The design was a modern, streamlined one in complete contrast to that of the cinema upstairs. A common paybox served both Studios with steps down to Studio Two on the right as one entered from Oxford Street. This was the West End's first twin cinema.

War-time conditions closed both screens for a while in late 1940 but they re-opened on 13 March 1941. When newsreels faded out, the addition of more cartoons continued to draw appreciative audiences from the throng of shoppers outside (there were also many family-type Disney films shown upstairs).

In 1983, Studio Two became Studio 4 in the Star circuit's four-screen complex following the tripling of the old Studio One. As noted in the section on Studio One, all four cinemas were closed on 8 December 1984.

1936
Monseigneur News Theatre
Jacey Leicester Square
Queen's House, Leicester Square

The ground floor entrance lobby of the former Queen's Hotel was adapted by Cecil Masey into a 350-seat news theatre for the Monseigneur circuit. With its excellent location just along from the Empire, it had little difficulty attracting custom from passers-by. After Jacey took over the Monseigneurs in June 1960, it became the Jacey Cartoon Theatre and then went over to "adult" feature programming with *Weird Weirdo* on 16 April 1970. It continued in that vein until closing on 24 June 1978. It subsequently became a shopping arcade until the entire building was gutted in the middle of 1983 for reconstruction behind the old facade.

The area occupied by the cinema is now a Highland Steak House.

☐ Below, as MONSEIGNEUR NEWS THEATRE but now showing cartoons, circa Christmas 1956. Above, as JACEY LEICESTER SQUARE with sex features, circa 1977 *(ph: Keith Skone)*.

☐ **STUDIO TWO in 1936** *(ph: John Maltby)*.

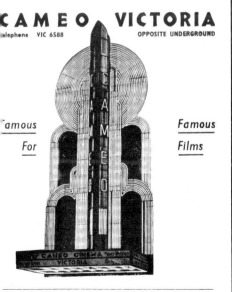

CAMEO VICTORIA
Telephone VIC 6588   OPPOSITE UNDERGROUND

Famous   Famous
For   Films

CAMEO CINEMA
VICTORIA

SEPTEMBER - 1959

'PICTURES ADD PLEASURE TO LIVING'

11 December 1936
Cameo
Classic
152 Victoria Street, Victoria

Even though Victoria already had a news theatre inside the railway station, the Cameo circuit of Clavering and Rose opened up this second news theatre opposite the Underground station and used the same architect, Alister G. MacDonald. It had a very narrow entrance, formerly occupied by Odone's Restaurant (which had supplied the catering for the Metropole cinema almost next door). Above this entrance was a vivid neon display in various colours with the name of the cinema as its central feature. This ensured that no-one overlooked the Cameo's existence. A long passage led to the back left-hand corner of the auditorium (the right-hand side of this passage was railed off as a holding area when the house was full). There were 604 seats in the spacious, well-raked auditorium. This was free-standing with exits onto Allington Road behind, and the left side wall lay directly adjacent to the back wall of the Metropole's auditorium (the auditoria were at right angles to each other). The Cameo's decoration was fairly plain, with combed plaster surfaces, two decorative grilles to each side of the screen, and concealed lighting from a long trough in the centre of the ceiling.

The Cameo later became a repertory cinema with two changes of programme weekly, on Sundays and Thursdays. Unlike the Biograph with its double bills, the Cameo's shows were kept as short as possible, consisting of a single feature film and trailers, with a cartoon if time allowed. The entire programme could run as little as 1hr. 45mins., and the feature was usually screened seven times daily. The first showing took place between 10.45am and 11.15am, and there would be three evening shows at around 5.45, 7.35 and 9.20pm. (On Sundays the Cameo couldn't open before 4.20pm and only managed three showings.) Occasionally, a longer film would reduce the number of screenings to as few as five, while really short films were run eight times. Foreign films with X certificates were shown once or twice a month, and Technicolor pictures were comparatively rare.

By keeping the programme short, there was more likelihood of luring in the busy traveller (in those days, many patrons quite happily came in during the middle of a film – a clock in the foyer showed the present time and the time you would leave if you came in at that moment). Although some patrons seemed surprised that the shows were so short, the policy was very successful during the 1950s. Seat prices in 1953-56

□ **Two shots of the CAMEO VICTORIA's auditorium in 1936, and front of monthly programme showing the eye-catching neon display above the canopy which helped compensate for the narrow entrance.**

□ **Plain exterior as CLASSIC in 1970's** *(ph: Keith Skone).*

were one shilling for the front rows, and two shillings and threepence for the centre and rear seats. Queues for the cheaper seats were very frequent in the evening as the extra cost of the better seats was prohibitive for many pockets.

The Cameo circuit was taken over by Classic in August 1967. The Cameo was renamed the Classic on 14 April 1972. The colourful neon sign disappeared and, as a lesser part of a larger chain, the cinema no longer seemed to be run with much enthusiasm or flair. The Rank Organisation had acquired the freehold and purchased the remainder of the lease from Classic in April 1973, then sublet the cinema back to the circuit. It became a first-run venue, showing some foreign films like *Le Deuxième Souffle*, but it was too out of the way to command top-drawing attractions. It then switched to weekly changes of mainstream double-bills and closed on Sunday 21 September 1980 with *Death Wish* and *The Warriors*.

The premises were leased from Rank for retail use from 7 August 1981 and used by Dickie Dirts for a short while as a cut-price jeans emporium. Rank sold the combined auditoria space of the Classic and Metropole off to a developer who has replaced them with the Allington Towers office block. The entrance to the Cameo/Classic has become the Victoria Prima-Pasta restaurant.

21 January 1937
Lansdowne News Theatre
Berkeley
Lansdowne Row, Mayfair

This subterranean newsreel theatre filled in vacant space that had been left underneath Lansdowne House, a new block of luxury flats and shops. (A gambling club has occupied the space under the Berkeley Square forecourt which would have made a far more prominent place for a cinema.) According to one trade figure of the time, the news theatre only had one means of escape, through the entrance, and it was surprising the authorities permitted it to open.

There were 277 seats in bright green upholstery. The architects were Wimperis, Simpson and Guthrie. The entrance was on narrow Lansdowne Row near the Berkeley Street end but hardly very conspicuous.

The County circuit agreed to lease the theatre in August 1936 and opened it to the public on the following 22 January after a private show the previous night. There was too little casual trade in the area to sustain a newsreel policy (all seats were one shilling) and it quickly flopped. In mid-March a repertory feature policy was inaugurated at higher prices beginning with *It Happened One Night*, and changed weekly. County next tried

re-launching it as an art cinema under the new name of the Berkeley with even higher prices (2s.6d. to 8s.6d.), beginning on Wednesday 23 June 1937 with Emil Jannings in *Der Herrscher* and employing a manager with the suitably commanding name of Count Ostrorog.

Foreign films were unfamiliar territory to County and Elsie Cohen of the Academy arrived to programme the Berkeley from April 1938. She had some success with films like *La Femme du Boulanger* which had a good run from June 1939 but the outbreak of war hit business so badly it closed in late November 1939 with a Fernandel comedy, *Ignace*, never to re-open as a cinema.

At the end of 1983 the place was closed, having been a club of some sort (with Arabic lettering and the name Titanic displayed). The whole of Lansdowne House has now been demolished and rebuilt, although Lansdowne Row survives.

☐ The LANSDOWNE in 1937.

4 February 1937
Gaumont
Haymarket

The complete internal reconstruction of the former Capitol (see 1925) to the plans of Gaumont-British's chief architect W. E. Trent involved the entrance being moved from the north-east corner of the island site to occupy the full width of the frontage onto Haymarket, where the entrance to the Kitkat Club had been. However, the Gaumont sign and the announcement of the current attraction were left on the old corner to face the bustling crowds at the top end of the street near Piccadilly Circus.

The new interior design was very much simpler than the old, but Trent somewhat surprisingly used a vertical emphasis in what was a narrow auditorium. The main decorative features were the life-size sculpted nude figures (a female above a male) on each side of the proscenium arch which were illuminated by concealed lighting. (A further nude figure, designed by Sigmund Pillitzer, was etched in glass for a foyer alcove.) There was more indirect lighting in an oval dome in front of the screen and from stepped coves across the ceiling.

A Compton organ was installed with the console on a plinth which emerged from the righthand side wall below the statuettes. The new stalls floor was 12ft.

☐ GAUMONT (formerly CAPITOL) HAYMARKET in 1937 *(ph: John Maltby)*.

lower than the old, taking up the space formerly occupied by the Kitkat Club. The old steeply-raked upper balcony was eliminated by the new ceiling. The total seating capacity was 1,328.

The Gaumont cinema was opened with G.-B.'s film *The Great Barrier* at a Royal premiere attended by Queen Mary. It was she who caused consternation by expressing a desire to attend the premiere of *The Wicked Lady* when that opened here for an exclusive run on 19 November 1945. An operator stood by in the projection box to turn down the sound and make some of the bawdier dialogue less audible. Fortunately, Queen Mary was impressed and told J. Arthur Rank, "A very good film—and a fine moral!"

Later in the Forties, the Gaumont was generally linked with the distant Marble Arch Pavilion to provide dual runs of new programmes until the Pavilion was leased out in 1952. With the Odeon and Gaumont circuits under joint control, the Gaumont tended to fare badly compared to the larger Odeons at Leicester Square and Marble Arch and the Leicester Square Theatre. The Rank Organisation declared that it lost around £100,000 between 1949 and 1956, only making a small profit in one year—1955—when noticeably more had been paid in film rental, suggesting better pictures were booked. In 1957, Rank sought planning permission to replace the Gaumont with offices and a new basement luxury cinema, stating that an average of only 400 people were attending performances in the 1,300 seat cinema. Approval was won on appeal.

On 5 February 1959 the Gaumont started a run of the Royal Performance film *The Horse's Mouth* after the premiere at the Empire. Shortly after, it closed following the run of a routine western *The Hangman* (21 May to 10 June 1959). The new Odeon Haymarket replaced it, opening in 1962.

☐ Above, two views of the GAUMONT's auditorium in 1937 and crowds outside in August 1958. Left, Henry Croudson at the Compton console *(courtesy of Tony Moss)*.

23 October 1937
Classic
96–100 Baker Street

Sam Seeman's Classic circuit was established at Croydon, Dalston, Hendon, Notting Hill Gate (Embassy), Sydenham, Tooting (two cinemas) and Portsmouth when he decided to build the first new cinema specifically constructed for repertory programming. The architects J. S. C. (Stanley) Beard and Bennett devised an intimate auditorium of 489 seats, including a balcony of approximately 180 seats. Streamlined towards the screen, with a reverse rake in the stalls, the Classic was exceptionally comfortable with excellent sightlines and impeccable presentation. The opening attraction on Saturday 23 October before an invited audience (the public were admitted from the following day) was a revival of *Mr. Deeds Goes to Town*. Shows ran from midday to midnight with only one feature and a maximum stay of a week. Stalls were one shilling and the circle two shillings. Changes were twice weekly from May 1940.

This was very much the flagship theatre

of the circuit, with head office installed next door, and standards were rigorously maintained. Space was very cramped on the stairs and in the toilets but this was the only drawback apart from the slight wear on the prints shown. In the Sixties, the Classic was even to be found pioneering new projection techniques with the operator sitting at a console board to the front left of the circle monitoring the semi-automatic projection tried out there.

While the Classic was controlled by the Laurie Marsh Group, the Baker Street freehold was sold with planning consent for a figure stated to be over £2 million; apparently the local planning authorities were delighted to see the place go as it enabled them to have the Georgian facade restored where the Classic's architects had dared to interrupt it and replacement cinemas were promised as part of the redevelopment.

The Classic closed on 24 March 1973 after a revival of *Straw Dogs*. Today Underwoods, the chemists, occupy most of the ground floor while two basement mini-cinemas, now known as the Screen on Baker Street, were opened in 1978.

□ **CLASSIC BAKER STREET in 1972** *(courtesy of former GLC Historic Buildings Division).*

2 November 1937
Odeon Leicester Square
23–27 Leicester Square

It was Oscar Deutsch who finally sealed the fate of the Alhambra music hall at the beginning of January 1936 when he made arrangements to build the Odeon flagship cinema on its site. Earlier, the Alhambra had been reported sold in May 1933 and scheduled to close on 20 August of that year to become a £750,000 Palace of Amusement (at one point to be named the New Century) with a dance floor, beer garden, garden restaurant, gymnasium, swimming bath and solarium, for which the architect was Edward A. Stone. Finally Oswald Stoll sold the theatre to Odeon and it closed on 1 September 1936. The *Othello* sequences for the United Artists picture *Men Are Not Gods* were filmed there on Sunday 8 October and it was demolished in November. The cost of the Odeon's site, which included the adjacent Turkish baths, was circa £550,000.

For this cinema only the best was good enough and the circuit's supervising architect Harry Weedon directly joined forces with one of the London-area Odeon designers, Andrew Mather, to produce a suitable scheme. An impressive plan was devised by Horace Ward in Mather's office and drawings were published, showing a tower where there is now a side passageway, a recessed frontage, and large areas of glass and light facing material. Oscar Deutsch and his colleagues fretted and argued over the design to the point where in March 1937 they all bundled into a seven-seat Daimler and went off to a London park with a shorthand typist and secretary to thrash it out in peace and quiet.

The final solution (said to be mainly the work of another Mather staff member, Thomas Braddock) was to make the Odeon the opposite of the rest of the circuit by dropping the use of yellow faience tiles and putting up 200 polished slabs of black granite each 6ft. x 5ft., with a 120ft. high tower to carry the name of the theatre, the whole to be outlined at night by neon in the tradition of German 'night architecture'. The rear of the site came out on Charing Cross Road where the Alhambra had had a secondary entrance; Odeon decided to have a 40ft. deep, ten storey high office block built there (principal architect: Eric Lyons), partly to produce additional revenue, partly to hide the stage end. However, it was possible to put up the name of the theatre and current programme over the passageway that had to be included between Charing Cross Road and Leicester Square along the side of the building. The office block was named Alhambra House.

The cost of constructing the Odeon was about five times the cost per seat of most Odeons, amounting to £232,755. The time taken was seven months. The exterior had two bronze canopies and a huge recess with discreet horizontal bars across the front on which neon lettering was

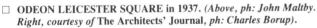

☐ **ODEON LEICESTER SQUARE in 1937.** *(Above, ph: John Maltby. Right, courtesy of* **The Architects' Journal**, *ph: Charles Borup).*

mounted. There was also originally a travelling sign under the lower canopy 37ft. long which announced the programme.

If the exterior was commanding and aloof, the auditorium was a wonderfully inviting achievement. There were 2,116 seats (1,140 in the stalls and 976 in the circle). The ceiling was crossed by bands of fibrous plaster which carried on down the side walls of the circle and which had shallow coves for lighting and ventilation. As each film ended, the cinema would light up from the semi-circular coves just above the screen opening, then from each of the coves in sequence to the back. The lights would dim in reverse sequence before the curtains parted.

A striking decorative feature was introduced on each of the front side walls of four naked figures plunging off a wave-like upwards extension of the wood-panelled dado, the impression of movement emphasised by curved bands in the plasterwork, like ripples. These were back-lit by concealed lighting and were the work of Raymond Britton Riviere.

A Compton organ, with its console lit up from within by changing colours, was installed. There was an orchestra pit which could be raised level with the stage to enlarge it. The theatre was equipped for full stage use with a safety curtain. The organ console could be raised even higher

and rotated so that the organist faced the audience. The seats were in a striking leopard-skin pattern unique to the theatre: more than one small boy was impressed by the thought of hundreds of leopards being hunted specially for the Odeon! The cinema was the last word in modernity and comfort.

With a tie-in to United Artists, the Odeon had access to prime product, beginning with *The Prisoner of Zenda*. Its only real rival to the number one spot was the Empire across the square. (When Royal Command Film Performances started, they generally alternated between the two theatres until the Empire closed and have since been solely at the Odeon.)

A Deutsch subsidiary, Scophony Ltd., put in a special 16ft. screen on which were shown television pictures live, projected 20ft. from behind. On 24 May 1939, the Derby was shown as it happened; on the next day, a fight was presented direct from Harringay Arena. This use of television was stopped by the war.

The Odeon escaped crippling damage during the hostilities but when a landmine dropped on Leicester Square around 20 October 1940 the vestibule, foyer, roof and part of the auditorium were badly affected and the Odeon was closed for a month for emergency repairs, re-opening on 18 November 1940 with *Hired Wife*. It

was not until 1948 that the damage could be fully remedied and then the Odeon shut for six weeks, re-opening on 30 December with *Scott of the Antarctic*.

Britain's first wide screen was installed here on 14 May 1953 for *Tonight We Sing*, beating the Empire by nine days. Then the really wide screen of CinemaScope made its public debut in this country at the Odeon when *The Robe* opened on 19 November 1953.

On 20 September 1967, after the premiere run of *Two for the Road*, the Odeon closed for an ill-conceived £200,000 modernisation scheme. The re-opening film on 28 December summed up what had happened with its title *Smashing Time*. All the original character of the building inside had gone—for ever. A new advertising lightbox had been installed just above the entrance outside, looking as though it had slipped from the recess higher up. New red, orange and mauve seating was introduced inside and unforgivably the leaping figures on the side walls had disappeared in favour of a smoothed over surface from the circle front forward. The subtle cove lighting scheme was banished. At least the Compton remained for occasional use.

Even at Rank, people seemed to regret what had happened. Rumours circulated that the figures could and would be retrieved from underneath the covering of

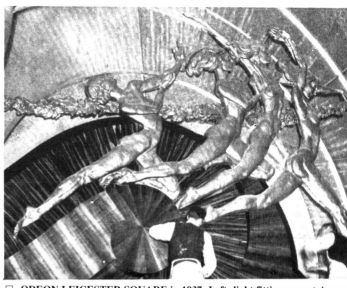

□ ODEON LEICESTER SQUARE in 1937. Left, light fitting over staircase to circle (*courtesy of* The Architects' Journal, *ph: Charles Borup*). Above, making final touches to one of the figures on the auditorium side walls prior to opening. Below, general view of the auditorium *(ph: John Maltby)*

plaster. An absurd fountain-like decorative feature in low relief was introduced on the side walls to relieve the plainness.

On 19 November 1975, the Odeon closed for £60,000 of further alterations, reopening on 18 December. New decorative features had been put on the side walls with a simple rolling form that recalled the original figures. These were picked out by spotlights during intervals.

Despite the general trend to multiple screens and mass openings, the Odeon has been retained as a single large cine-ma specialising in exclusive runs (at least for the central West End area). In the summer of 1990, even a hit attraction like *Dick Tracy* had a two week run before opening anywhere else.

In 1987, it was extensively modernised. The black glass exterior was restored to shine with something like its original brilliance, and the advertising panel was raised to fit the front of the large recess, opening up a view of Leicester Square once again from windows in the circle lounge. New seating and carpeting were installed, while a new treatment of the side walls introduced long wavy strips of vertical neon that light up and fade in sequence.

In 1990, as described in more detail later on, five new screens were added in the former side passage and called the Odeon Mezzanine.

☐ Above, ODEON's auditorium to rear. Note projection box over rear circle. Below, the ODEON by night in 1937 *(ph: John Maltby)*.

25 November 1937
Ritz
Empire 2
Leicester Square

The Ritz was intended to be another large news theatre for Clavering and Rose, like their Cameo Victoria opened the previous year. The architect was George Coles and it was in basement space within a new office block (architects: Wimperis, Simpson and Guthrie) that had a Dolcis shoe shop on the ground floor. It was to have been known as the Rendezvous or State News Theatre.

The entrance was directly alongside that of the Empire whose owners, Metro-Goldwyn-Mayer, decided that it would make an excellent house to continue runs of films from their big cinema. And so the new hall, with a seating capacity of 430 on one floor, was taken over by MGM before opening and named the Ritz. Its tiny vestibule had a striking figure of a nude five foot high sand-blasted in glass and lit by concealed lighting. The auditorium was heated by electric storage radiators. Seats were in soft pink against blue carpet.

The main problem with the Ritz has always been the very poor sightlines from the slight rake. The screen couldn't be raised because of the low ceiling which

□ **The RITZ with new canopy in 1953.**

also created an oppressive feeling. These defects wouldn't have mattered so much for a quick visit to an hour of cartoons and newsreels as originally planned. Fortunately the Ritz had such top-grade product from the Empire (though it also premiered weaker MGM titles) and was

so well located that it generally did well. Its programmes were mainly advertised as a footnote to those for the Empire.

The Ritz enjoyed the distinction of opening *Gone with the Wind* simultaneously with the Empire and Palace Theatre on 18 April 1940. (Being

□ **The RITZ. Top, the small but stylish entrance hall in 1937 with stairs to auditorium below. Bottom, two views of auditorium, left in 1937, right after 1970 modernisation.** *(Left two photos courtesy of* The Architects' Journal, *right top from BFI Stills, Posters and Designs collection.)*

16ft. below ground, it had been envisaged as an air raid shelter, but was spared to become one of London's safer war-time venues.) *GWTW* was withdrawn from the Ritz after 23 May 1940 but returned (when the Empire discontinued its run) from 11 July 1940 and remained there until 8 June 1944, the second longest run in a single West End cinema.

The other lengthy run at the Ritz occurred with *Quo Vadis*, the MGM epic which opened there and at the Carlton in a joint European premiere on Friday 25 January 1952 and ran at the Leicester Square cinema until 20 May 1953.

In 1970 the Ritz was modernised with the round aisle supporting pillars being boxed in square, the rows of seating staggered to improve sightlines, and the capacity reduced from 414 to 393. The cinema closed on Sunday 19 April for the work to be carried out (architects: Sidney Kaye, Eric Firmin and Partners) and re-opened on 21 May.

On 9 November 1972 the Ritz was renamed Empire Two. The following year it was taken over by Cinema International Corporation, the new distributors of MGM films, and reverted back to being the Ritz.

Further alterations were carried out in 1978 and it re-opened in July with 350 seats. On 27 May 1982 it once again became Empire 2. From being tiny in the Thirties, it has become a medium-size theatre in the Eighties, playing a mixture of first runs and follow-ons. The original entrance has been turned into an ice-cream parlour, and patrons have a detour through Empire 1 to reach the auditorium. Tickets are sold at the box-office in the Empire 1 entrance hall and Empire 2 is reached by ascending the stairs and turning back to the left to connect up with the original staircase.

12 October 1938
Warner
Warner West End
& Rendezvous
Warner West End
1, 2, 3, 4 and 5
Cranbourne Street

After the Empire music hall and the Alhambra it was the turn of Daly's Theatre to bite the dust to make way for a super cinema. Warner Bros. acquired the legitimate theatre in August 1937 and it closed on 25 September of that year. The Warner Theatre was built on an enlarged site that included space obtained along Lisle Street. The architects were Edward A. Stone and T. R. Somerford.

The striking frontage was faced in reconstructed marble blocks chemically treated to preserve a warm cream colour. Sculptured plaques by Bainbridge Copnall representing the spirit of sight and sound were placed high on each side of the facade. A tower feature carrying the name of the theatre rose vertically from a curved high recess.

The Warner's auditorium was simple, pleasant and unassuming, more like an average suburban circuit house, but with a striking preponderance of green. The side walls and front of the circle were covered in squares of acoustic "quilting" to absorb sound. There was a Compton organ.

The new cinema opened with Warners' big-budget Technicolor costume adventure set in Merrie England, *The Adventures of Robin Hood*. The stalls seated 1,169 and the circle 620 for a total of 1,789. With its pick of the Warner studio output and its excellent location just off Leicester Square next to the Hippodrome, the Warner has always been one of the West End's most prosperous cinemas.

Redecoration occurred in 1957 leaving the auditorium walls predominantly Munsel red and the seats re-upholstered in peacock blue. By this time, seating was down slightly to 1,565 (most cinemas lost a few rows of seats at the front when CinemaScope was installed because sightlines were so bad). Instead of leaving well alone, the Warner succumbed to a

□ **The WARNER Leicester Square in 1938** *(courtesy of* **The Architects' Journal***)*.

total interior modernisation scheme costing £110,000, for which it was closed from Monday 13 April until 23 July 1964 when it re-opened with *Robin and the Seven Hoods* and a new seating capacity of 1,460. A new ceiling, new seating, and wall-to-wall curtains were installed along with a new screen for 70mm. The result was paralysingly bland and uninteresting.

Less than six years later, it was gone. The Warner closed on 31 January 1970 for a twinning scheme. Re-opening took place on 29 October of that year when the 890-seat Warner West End opened upstairs, followed on 12 November by the 686-seat Warner Rendezvous downstairs. Warners had learned a lesson and the ceilings of the new cinemas were used decoratively to relieve the plainness. In the West End (later the Warner 2), 400 glass-fibre drums of varying size were attached to the ceiling, some containing light bulbs for illumination. In place of the traditional screen curtains, a decorative 20ft. metalwork open panel slid in half to reveal the screen (this is now replaced by conventional curtains). In the Rendezvous, there were no curtains either, with the screen merging into white wing walls, while there were clusters of overhead lights on a dark ceiling. The architect for the reconstruction was Leslie C. Norton, the designer was Felix Holton, and the decor was by Alan Best.

On 29 September 1974, the Warner Rendezvous was renamed the Warner West End 2 and the former bar opened as the Warner West End 3, seating 132 and served by a separate entrance to the side of the main doors.

Warners realised that two large cinemas were insufficiently flexible and so the Warner West End 2 (ex-Warner Rendezvous) was closed for twinning. It re-opened on 20 November 1975 as the Warner West End 3 and 4, seating 270 and 434. The former 1 & 3 screens were re-numbered 2 & 1 respectively. A new 180-seat Warner West End 5 was opened in disused space in October 1981. A new paybox serves all five screens. A labyrinth of narrow passages brings patrons to the remoter screens.

To sum up this necessarily confusing story, the Warner in early 1991 has five screens, seating (in numerical order) 132, 890, 246, 434 and 105. The spacious number 2 screen is one of the best in the West End, while the very wide number 1 screen is one of the most awkward. The others fall somewhere between.

In mid-1990, Warner Bros. was thinking of adding two further screens on the roof of the Warner but more recently the company has submitted schemes for planning approval that would involve the demolition of the entire building behind the existing façade and the construction of a new seven-screen complex.

☐ **Three shots inside the WARNER Leicester Square in 1938** *(courtesy of* **The Architects' Journal***).*

□ Left, the new look inside the WARNER from April 1964: new seating, 70mm screen and wall-to-wall curtains. Below, part of the next new look inside the WARNER: this is the WARNER WEST END, later WARNER 2, with its distinctive ceiling drums, essentially an extension of the original cinema's circle.

□ The upper part of the WARNER WEST END's frontage in 1991 with the two facing figures sculptured by Bainbridge Copnall, and general view of the exterior *(ph: Allen Eyles)*.

7 December 1938
Topical News Theatre
Time News Theatre
Times
Jaceyland
Times Centa 1 & 2
Cannon 1 & 2 Baker Street
Approach Road, Baker Street Station

Newsreel theatres had been built inside Victoria and Waterloo Stations but this was the first and only one put up in part of an Underground Station. The main entrance, set back from Marylebone Road, was picked out in a vivid neon display but there was also access from one of the station booking halls.

The 306-seat single-floor cinema was designed by Leslie C. Norton for a company headed by Jack Davis who ran the Monseigneur News Theatres. The Baker Street station master performed the opening ceremony. It was proclaimed that news items photographed by amateurs would be included in the programmes.

Then known as the Topical News Theatre, it was renamed the Time News Theatre circa 1942. The Jacey group acquired this along with the Monseigneurs in June 1960 and it became the Times Cinema with a feature film policy from 9 April 1967, beginning with a two-month season of ballet and opera pictures. It closed for redecoration by October of that year and re-opened as the Jaceyland with a revival of Disney's *The Living Desert* in late November. It closed on Sunday 27 October 1968 to re-open the following Thursday as the Times Cinema under the direction of the eccentric distributor and film-maker Antony Balch, beginning with revivals of *Witchcraft Through the Ages* and *Un Chien Andalou* in a double-bill.

The burgeoning Cinecenta group took the place over from 1 May 1972 and renamed it the Times Centa, closing it on 1 November that year for an £80,000 twinning. A dividing wall was built down the middle of the auditorium creating two long narrow cinemas seating 171 and 169 which opened as Times Centa 1 & 2 on 15 March 1973. They have operated mainly with revival double-bills, clocking up some extraordinarily long runs (two years with *Cabaret*). Star took over the Cinecenta circuit in December 1979 and continued to operate the Times Centa screens in much the same way. Since then, Cannon have taken over Star and the cinemas were renamed the Cannon Baker Street on Friday 6 December 1985. Then, from Friday 21 November 1986, they were briefly renamed Premiere 2 and an art film policy (comparable to that at Premiere 1 at the Swiss Centre) was introduced with *Thérèse* on screen 1 and *A Passage to India* on screen 2. They soon reverted to being the Cannon Baker Street and have moved to mainstream first-run attractions. Thanks to their distance from the main West End houses and despite their small size, these two screens have been opening smash hits like *Indiana Jones and the Last Crusade* concurrent with the Empire and other major West End cinemas.

22 February 1939
Monseigneur News Theatre
Jacey Marble Arch
523 Oxford Street

The basement of British Industries House, adjacent to the Marble Arch Pavilion, was the last of the sites located by the Monseigneur circuit for a news theatre, and again it was a shrewd choice in a busy shopping area at the end of Oxford Street where it would be sure to attract shoppers for a hour's rest and relaxation. The £50,000 scheme was drawn up by Leslie C. Norton in conjunction with Cecil Masey and provided for a 400-seat auditorium with a café and (in the original plans, at least) a processing laboratory for specially shot news films.

Following a performance for invited guests only on Wednesday 22nd, the Monseigneur opened to the public the following day with the large screen television presentation of a boxing match between Boon and Danahan, using its Scophony installation.

The Jacey group took over the Monseigneur circuit in the early Sixties and renamed this cinema the Jacey. A switch to feature films was inaugurated in 1965. This began as mainly X certificate sex films but many Hollywood commercial films and special family attractions were also screened, more than at other Jaceys. Perhaps this reflected great difficulties in attracting audiences for the Jacey didn't last long, closing in mid-December 1967 with a foreign double-X revival bill, *Galia* plus *Who Wants to Sleep?*

The premises were then converted into a shopping mall called the Jacey Art Gallery which had closed down at the end of 1983. Eight years later, the entrance area at least is occupied by a branch of Pizza Hut.

☐ **Auditorium of TOPICAL NEWS THEATRE in 1938 and exterior as TIMES CENTA in 1984** *(latter ph: Allen Eyles).*

20 April 1939
Paris
4–12 Lower Regent Street
(Rex House)

The Paris art cinema was situated two storeys below street level in the Rex House redevelopment. The architect for the entire scheme was Robert Cromie who had originally been engaged in 1936 to design two live theatres for the site when it was to be the London Theatre Centre. By 1937 the idea of two cinemas had been substituted, along with a restaurant, shops and six floors of offices. The promoters were headed by Harry Lane and Stuart Doyle, an Australian entertainment czar who envisaged a counterpart to the State Sydney complex. By 1938, this idea had been abandoned and a single cinema, then to be known as the Regent, and a restaurant with balcony had been decided upon.

The Marquis de Casa Maury arranged to take the cinema as a sister to his Curzon. Perhaps for this reason it has a striking simplicity of design reminiscent of the Mayfair building as it then was. The walls were in rough-texture plaster toned off-white; all the lighting was indirect; and the only colouring was provided by the bright red seats, carpet and dado.

The Paris opened with Jean Renoir's *La Bête Humaine*. It had 550 seats on one floor. *Hôtel du Nord* and *Hostages* followed before the policy was put aside for English-speaking revivals. The outbreak of war hindered its progress and it closed in late November 1939 shortly after the Curzon. It did re-open on 1 February 1940 but functioned only irregularly until by summer it was being used solely for trade shows. Then in September of that year it was requisitioned by the Office of Works, never to operate as a public cinema again. In June 1941 it was reported that the company which had operated it as a cinema owed £63,000 to the landlord in rent and had £1,500 further liabilities.

But the Paris still found a rosy future and it survives in mid-1991 with its old name, really very little altered (the cove lighting of the foyer ceiling still in use, the auditorium only slightly modified) as the BBC Paris Studios where radio programmes are recorded before live audiences, the deep location helping to eliminate extraneous noises.

☐ **The PARIS in 1939** *(top three ph: John Maltby, above courtesy of* **The Architects' Journal***, ph: Charles Borup).*

25 September 1939
Embassy
194 Tottenham Court Road

The Embassy was designed by George Coles for Montague Cohen and Arnold Michaels to occupy the old premises of Heal's store which had moved next door. The cinema had a narrow entrance on Tottenham Court Road. The facade was in terra cotta framed by green neon strip lighting while the current film programme was announced in red letters set at the front of a series of back-illuminated troughs. The auditorium, seating 782 on a single floor, was at right angles to the entrance with the screen end backing onto Torrington Place.

The cinema cost £45,000 and was envisaged as another outlet for foreign films. It was claimed that special attention had been given to the rake and that 200 seats had been sacrificed to ensure that every patron had a clear view of the screen and especially the bottom where the subtitles would appear. It was also planned to install equipment for receiving television transmissions for large screen presentation.

An early September opening was delayed by the outbreak of war and the temporary closure of all cinemas. The Embassy finally opened on Monday 25 September with films like *Hôtel du Nord*. The programming policy quickly became very eclectic with weekly changes of foreign revivals and move-overs, Hollywood double-bills, foreign and Hollywood films together (the latter a common practice elsewhere).

Like many others, the Embassy closed temporarily at the height of the Blitz in late September 1940. It was badly damaged, along with Heal's, by a German air raid on the night of 14/15 October 1940 and it never re-opened. The cinema's site is now swallowed up by the northward extension of Heal's. It was the shortest-lived of all the later West End cinemas, although the Paris had a shorter life as a cinema.

□ **Below, in the view of Tottenham Court Road looking south, the EMBASSY with its broad canopy is indicated by a black pointer. In lower picture, the EMBASSY is partly obscured, next to Heal's, "closed until further notice"** *(courtesy of Tony Moss).*

15 January 1940
Cinephone
London News Theatre
Cinephone
421 Oxford Street/Lumley Street

The Cinephone was a conversion of part of the existing Keysign House from shops and basement into another outlet for foreign films. The location was a little curious, with the cinema out on its own between Bond Street and Marble Arch. It was the first British theatre of a company headed by a Mr. Nakhinoff who ran seven cinemas in Brussels and one in Paris. His architect was R. Jelinek-Karl, who made the best out of a very awkward site.

The result was a long, narrow auditorium with 382 seats downstairs and 76 seats in the small balcony at ground level (a total of 458). The projection room was at first floor level.

Plans were passed in January 1939 but the cinema didn't open until a year later after war had been declared. It closed in mid-September 1940 when air raids made conditions impossible, and it didn't re-open. (A Nazi-banned film *Fall of a Tyrant* and a one-week revival of Hollywood's *House of Seven Gables* seem to have been the last attractions, the latter ending on 21 September.) The cinema was requisitioned by the Ministry of Works for storage use in 1941.

It then lay empty until the Jacey circuit acquired it early in the Fifties but it was two year before they could re-open it in February 1953 as the London News Theatre with 459 seats, operating from 11am daily.

It went over to a foreign film policy and reverted to being the Cinephone from 21 October 1954 with *We, The Women* and continued in this vein until closure on 31 January 1973 with *Seven Times a Day* and *Unsatisfied Virgins*. Most of the films played were sensational (or made to seem so for publicity purposes) but an eclectic booking policy meant that some very good

□ **The CINEPHONE with its long, low auditorium stretching down Lumley Street** *(courtesy of John Fernee).*

□ **The CINEPHONE in 1939.** *(Left, both courtesy of John Fernee. Right, ph: John Maltby.)*

Continental pictures played here on occasion, such as *Dear John*. The auditorium was never ideal and it was impossible to fit an adequate size CinemaScope screen while the screen was always too distant from the balcony.

The site was a valuable one in the heart of the Oxford Street shopping area and after having been British Airways offices was in 1990 a jeans emporium called Lisa.

□ **Auditorium of the CINEPHONE.** *(Near left and above, ph: John Maltby.)*

30 September 1954
Casino Cinerama Theatre
Casino

Old Compton Street

This massive structure, built on the corner of two narrow Soho streets, Old Compton Street and Greek Street, opened on 3 April 1930 as the Prince Edward Theatre, designed by Edward Stone with interior decorations by Marc Henri and Laverdet. It was principally intended for live show use with its two balconies and 1,544 seats (plus seven boxes) but it was equipped for showing films and presented *Song O' My Heart* in May 1930.

□ Above, the CASINO in 1930's *(courtesy of Tony Moss)*. Right, the CASINO CINERAMA THEATRE in 1962 *(from BFI Stills, Posters and Designs collection)*. Below, the installation of Cinerama in 1954 *(courtesy of CTA Archive)*.

In fact, its principal use in the early Thirties was for film trade shows (daytime and evenings) and it became a public cinema briefly from 20 November 1933. It was reconstructed into the London Casino cabaret restaurant in 1936, closed during the Blitz and became a club for servicemen in 1942. It reverted to stage

shows after the war until it was selected to become the home of Cinerama.

Architects Frank Baessler and T. P. H. and E. Braddock drew up the plans for installing a deeply curved 64ft. wide by 23ft. high screen, a stereophonic sound system (five speakers behind the screen, others around the auditorium), and three

separate projection booths at the rear of the stalls to provide the three adjacent images that made up the Cinerama picture. Some stalls seating was inevitably lost and part of the upper circle had to be taken out of use because of the bad sightlines.

This Is Cinerama made its debut at the Casino Cinerama Theatre on 30 September 1954, two years to the day after its New York debut. There were 1,337 seats in 1956. The theatre prospered while films were forthcoming in the Cinerama process (other Cinerama installations took place at the Coliseum and Royalty to cope with the demand) but when the supply dried up in the Sixties it fell upon difficult times. Various 70mm films could be shown on the huge screen but even these were not plentiful. The upper circle was closed and seating fell to 1,127 by 1965.

The theatre was taken over by EMI from 4 May 1974 for dual use as a cinema and live theatre, and the Cinerama screen was removed as part of a modernisation scheme. The Casino ceased to be used for films after a revival double bill of *Lady Sings the Blues* and *Mahogany* ended on Saturday 8 April 1978. It then reverted to its original name of the Prince Edward Theatre and re-opened in June 1978 with the long-running stage musical *Evita*. The subsequent long runs of *Chess* and *Anything Goes* have helped put it firmly back on the theatrical map.

4 February 1959
Columbia
Classic Shaftesbury Avenue
Premiere
Curzon West End
93 Shaftesbury Avenue/Frith Street

The Columbia replaced the bombed Shaftesbury Pavilion of 1912; it is in the basement of the Wingate House redevelopment of the stretch of Shaftesbury Avenue between Frith Street and Greek Street. Harold Wingate already ran the Curzon and he engaged its architects—now Sir John Burnet, Tait and Partners—to design his new cinema. His original plan was to open it as the Paris, a sister art house to the Curzon, but while it was under construction to the plans of H. G. Hammond, Columbia Pictures arranged to lease it, making it the first cinema the company had ever operated anywhere in the world. Appropriately, it opened with the Columbia name, although the first attraction, *Gigi*, came from another studio, MGM. A policy of extended runs and separate performances with bookable seats had been determined, with audiences being spared screen advertising.

The cinema had a generous foyer, originally designed to accommodate queues for the advance booking office. The canopy had distinctive red or white lettering on a black background (regrettably abandoned in recent years for a conventional white background). Stairs lead to a mezzanine foyer where toilets, cloakroom (when in use) and a confectionery counter are established. The rear of the auditorium is reached down a further flight of stairs.

There were originally 734 seats on a single floor with the rear section enclosed by a wooden barrier as at the Curzon. Seats were staggered to improve the view of the screen past heads in front. The projection rake was only 4 degrees.

The low matte-black ceiling had random circular openings for ventilation and lighting. The projection equipment and screen were capable of taking 70mm and Todd AO films. There were two sets of curtains in front of the screen.

The main problem for the Columbia was a shortage of the kind of films it had been planned to show. The policy became eclectic. The big Columbia films generally went to larger, more centrally placed cinemas and the Columbia cinema was left resorting to a season of the studio's old Oscar winners like *It Happened One Night*. It also tried a tie-in with the Curzon, playing a dubbed print of a foreign film while the Curzon took the subtitled version.

In the Seventies, of course, films went into general release much more quickly and extended runs of big attractions at single cinemas virtually disappeared. When the Columbia shared in a multiple opening of a new Clint Eastwood film like *The Outlaw Josey Wales*, it could do excellent business but all too often it was showing left-over product.

Cannon Classic took over the cinema, closed it for a few days to install Dolby stereo and make other improvements, and re-opened it on Thursday 19 August 1982 as the Classic sharing in a multiple opening of *The Last American Virgin*. Since then its policy has been erratic, with a number of 70mm revivals. Then on Friday 9 March 1984 it became the Premiere and inaugurated an art house policy with *Love Streams*. This collapsed after a few months and the Premiere closed on Thursday 29 November 1984 after two matinee performances of its current attraction, a British thriller called *The Hit*.

By this time, Harold Wingate had died but his son Roger had inherited his enthusiasm for cinema and was controlling the Curzon along with the family property firm, Chesterfield Properties. Roger Wingate decided to turn the Premiere in-

☐ **The COLUMBIA in 1982, with main entrance top right, mezzanine foyer bottom right** (*all courtesy of the Museum of London*).

□ **The auditorium of the COLUMBIA in 1982** *(courtesy of the Museum of London, ph: John Edwards)*, **and (below) the drab exterior as the CURZON WEST END in March 1991** *(ph: Allen Eyles)*.

to a sister cinema to the Curzon, as his father had once envisaged. It re-opened as the Curzon West End on 8 March 1985 with *Weatherby* (the other Curzon now being called the Curzon Mayfair). A new screen was installed along with a Dolby sound system, and two sets of tabs remained in use, with red and green lighting. The low ceiling was repainted black again. The auditorium was recarpeted and the number of seats (which had by then been reduced to 702) was reduced further to 624 to provide greater leg room, while the enclosing barrier to the rear section was removed.

The Curzon West End generally plays different films from the Curzon Mayfair, specialising in exclusive first runs of arthouse pictures.

November 1960
Compton Cinema Club
The Londoner
60 Old Compton Street

The Compton opened deep in Soho and lived up to the image of the area with uncensored films for club members, beginning with the banned American production *Private Property*. It had 186 seats in a basement area. Projection was from behind and beneath the screen through mirrors onto a main mirror in front which reflected the picture onto the 12ft. wide screen.

In July 1977 the Compton varied its usual programming of obscure porn to open the banned Pasolini film *Salo—120 Days of Sodom* which was withdrawn after two week for fear of prosecution despite full houses. A brief period of public presentations occurred from August to November 1977.

On 13 March 1980 the Star group renamed it the Londoner and tried a complete change of image with a public season of Woody Allen revivals changed weekly. The Londoner reverted to hardcore programmes after October 1981 while retaining its new name. By early 1984, the premises had closed. There was some interest from the Paul Raymond Organisation in re-opening an 'adult' cinema here, while a novel scheme to showcase Russian pictures was contemplated by another entrepreneur. But in time the basement has become part of business premises, the canopy has long gone, and no trace of a cinema remains.

☐ **Queue at the COMPTON for *Paris Playgirls (from BFI Stills, Posters and Designs collection)* and 1960 view of the auditorium.**

4 June 1962
Odeon Haymarket
Haymarket/St. James's Market

The building which had housed the Capitol (1925) and Gaumont (1937) was completely gutted to become offices with a new cinema in the basement. Whereas the Capitol had had an entrance on the corner facing up Haymarket towards Piccadilly Circus and the Gaumont an entrance across the full Haymarket width of the site, the new Odeon has a minute foyer on the less favourable corner furthest down Haymarket. This contains an advance booking office and leads to a lift and stairs down to the mezzanine level (cloakroom, staff and manager's quarters) and then the stalls level (where toilets and sales kiosk are also located).

The architect was Leslie C. Norton and the Odeon's interior decoration was by Alan Best. The side walls were hung in Thai silk panels of gold and tan, while the ceiling of suspended fibrous plaster has circular holes creating a honeycomb effect. With wider-than-average seating and a warm, inviting appearance, the auditorium offers real luxury and comfort with a large screen and much more height than the Columbia. It seats 600 on one floor with the back rows stepped. Projection is level.

The opening attraction was Columbia's forgotten epic, *Barabbas*. Over the years, the Odeon has come to specialise in class or up-market attractions. Some random examples are Tati's *Playtime*, *Chariots of Fire*, *The French Lieutenant's Woman*, many of the Woody Allen films, and the Mel Gibson version of *Hamlet*. It remains a highly desirable venue for distributors with the kind of film that needs a

☐ **ODEON HAYMARKET, circa 1969** *(ph: Keith Skone)*.

□ **ODEON HAYMARKET auditorium in 1962** *(courtesy of* **The Architects' Journal***).*

slow build-up and is likely to benefit from good word of mouth. It is one of the few cinemas that usually still presents films on exclusive runs rather than as part of a multiple opening.

Empire
Empire 1
Empire 1 2 and 3
Leicester Square

The reconstruction of the Empire provided the veteran cinema architect George Coles with both his major post-war project and his swansong (he died a couple of years later). The building was split into two from the entrance inwards. The left hand half (facing the entrance) leads into the new Empire cinema which was constructed in roughly the position of the old circle on stadium lines with 1,330 seats and with the screen at the same end of the building as before. The right-hand half of the entrance admits to the Empire dance hall which is located downstairs where the stalls of the old Empire had been. (There have been problems of sound penetration from the dance hall.)

The long entrance hall and foyer (with its licensed bar and confectionery counter) are huge by post-war standards, partly using the space under the rear

□ **The EMPIRE. Restored exterior in 1991** *(ph: Keith Skone)*, **entrance stairs circa 1965.**

The lounge and bar area of the EMPIRE in 1962, with entrance to auditorium at left (*from BFI Stills, Posters and Designs collection*).

raised section of the cinema auditorium. The fan-shaped cinema seats 688 in the stalls and 642 in the rear. It offers the most spectacular and relaxing viewing arena of all the post-war additions to the West End. Concealed lighting in bands up the walls and across the ceiling changes colour during intervals. The carpeting and seats are a rich-red, the latter with a certain amount of 'give' that led to the unfounded suspicion on a first pre-opening visit that the bolts hadn't been properly tightened! There are two sets of curtains plus a fringing festoon curtain that lifts clear before the main curtains part in the centre.

When the Empire re-opened on Wednesday 19 June 1962 with the Metro musical *Jumbo*, the MGM company was in the doldrums and audience pullers were hard to find. The Empire failed to regain its old popularity until it gambled on reviving some old Garbo pictures in August 1963 and was rewarded with huge audiences, including near capacity attendances in the afternoon, to see the old classics in black and white on an old ratio screen! 18,000 admissions were recorded during a week's run of *Queen Christina*. Garbo revivals returned in November/December.

MGM sold the theatre when it withdrew from distribution to Cinema International Corporation in 1973. CIC now handled MGM pictures as well as Paramount and Universal product and were able to provide the Empire with the pick of the crop (*Grease* probably holds the attendance record: 31,689 admissions in a week). When the adjacent Ritz (also taken over) was re-named Empire 2, the main cinema became Empire 1. Storage space off the main foyer was then cleared to make room for an 80-seat Empire 3 which opened on Friday 29 November 1985 with *Witness*, moving over from Plaza 4.

In 1989 a £2 million improvement scheme was completed and the Empire billed itself as 'The World's Most Spectacular Movie Venue'. Early on, the original 1928 frontage was restored and returned to view, above a rather hideous new canopy shared with the adjacent ballroom. In the outer foyer with a computerised box-office, a bulkhead was raised to allow a glimpse of the inner foyer from the outside. The entire inner foyer was redesigned with a 40-screen video wall and a ceiling in which 13,500 fibre optic lenses give the impression of twinkling stars. The main auditorium was thankfully left intact, with the seating refurbished, a new THX sound system installed, and three sets of short laser shows prepared with different moods to precede the feature attraction, the one most appropriate to the film being used. The concealed lighting in the walls and ceiling is also used in conjuction with the lasers to create striking effects.

The spacious auditorium of the EMPIRE in 1984 with its bands of concealed lighting (*ph: Allen Eyles*).

9 May 1963
Circlorama
Classic Piccadilly Circus
Denman Street,
    then **Glasshouse Street**

This was a temporary cinema built at a cost of over £100,000 in less than seven weeks on the old Monico site for Leonard Urry and Leon Hepner to test the market appeal of a new system of completely circular cinema. Several hundred patrons could stand in the middle of a round space and look at eleven screens that filled the walls all round them while sound came from fifty-one speakers located behind the screen, on the ceiling, and below the floor. There were eleven narrow gaps between the screens from which projection beams emerged from eleven projectors; the effect was rather like looking out of windows past vertical bars.

The opening attraction was the Soviet *Russian Roundabout* and the twenty-minute shows ran at half-hourly intervals from noon to 10pm. The original entrance was in Denman Street but a much more conspicuous entrance was opened on Piccadilly Circus in the autumn of 1963. There was a hitch around this time when the second Circlorama feature sent over by the Russians wouldn't work on the projection system and the opening attraction had to be held over. However, *Circlorama Cavalcade* was the new presentation in 1964. The cinema closed the following year.

Classic took over and made it into a conventional cinema with 270 seats and one screen, re-opening it as the Classic on 10 April 1966 with a revival of Shirley Temple in *Rebecca of Sunnybrook Farm*. In later years, it generally played newer films, many of them sexploitation, and had many all-night shows. Undoubtedly, the biggest attraction was *Easy Rider*, which had its British premiere run here in 1969 and proved such a draw that it was played around the clock, the first time a British cinema had shown a film without any break.

It closed on 24 October 1976 for redevelopment of the site and the entrance to the Classic is now occupied by Burger King.

☐ **CLASSIC PICCADILLY CIRCUS in 1969** *(ph: Kevin S. Wheelan).*

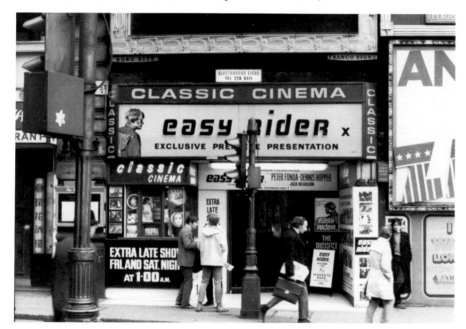

June 1965
Prince Charles
Leicester Place, Lisle Street

The Prince Charles opened as a live theatre on 26 December 1962, designed by Carl Fisher and Associates. It was dressed up as a music hall for revues but also put to film use in Spring 1964 with press shows and public and schools' morning and afternoon screenings of *Tartuffe* without interrupting its live evening performances. In August 1964 a three week season of film musicals was presented in the afternoons and early evenings before the music hall revue. There were 358 seats.

Full-time cinema use came in June 1965. Shortly after, on 4 July, the Northern-based Star Associated Holdings took it over as their first West End cinema. It now had 414 seats. If the cinema was anywhere near full, sightlines were dreadful and it was closed on 2 November 1968 for complete internal reconstruction, using the basement of the building to create a new stalls floor with a circle above. The architect for the conversion was Carlo S. Biskupek with interior design by Harold Bartram.

The new 631-seat auditorium was very plain and oddly shaped with a bend in one wall, while loud noises from outside (especially the sirens of police cars and ambulances) could be clearly heard. It had a screen curtain that opened from left to right instead of parting in the middle.

The Prince Charles re-opened with a spicy sex comedy *Benjamin* on Tuesday 21 January 1969 and became noted for long runs of this type of film – *Emmanuelle*, *Caligula*, etc.

☐ **The PRINCE CHARLES in March 1991** *(ph: Allen Eyles).*

It became the Cannon Prince Charles after Cannon took over the Star circuit in 1985 and was thoroughly refurbished by early 1986. There were new seats, Cannon circuit carpet, orange drapes with globe light fittings on the side walls, and the seating was cut to 488 and arranged in one central block in the stalls. The Prince Charles has proved difficult to programme successfully in recent years, especially with only one screen. It has been too close to the big West End houses to play the same films, yet a little too out of the way up a side street off Leicester Square to gain strong attractions on its own.

On 26 April 1991, Cannon handed over the Prince Charles to Robins Cinemas, providing this rapidly expanding chain with a West End foothold.

6 April 1966
Curzon
Curzon Mayfair
Hertford Street/Curzon Street, Mayfair

The architects of the original Curzon and the new Columbia were engaged to design the new Curzon within a £½m. block of flats and offices on the old cinema's site. The actual designer for Sir John Burnet, Tait and Partners was H.G. Hammond, who had been responsible for the Columbia. Unlike the Columbia and most postwar replacements, the Curzon has an auditorium on the first floor rather than in the basement and it seats more than its predecessor.

The entrance was moved around the corner off Curzon Street itself. The auditorium went to the other extreme from the old Curzon's stark simplicity with sculptured glass fibre murals, metallically finished, that helped disperse sound but gave a primitive, cave-like impression. The coffered ceiling contains lighting and stereophonic speakers.

The 530 seats are mounted on the edge

☐ The new CURZON as part of an office block in 1966 *(courtesy of* The Architects' Journal, *ph: Wm. J. Toomey).*

of the steppings rather than on standards; there are six additional seats in two private boxes overhead in the rear corners. Seating is in a stadium

☐ The auditorium of the CURZON with its large screen set for Academy ratio. Raised carpeted area near camera covers entrance with steps up either side between front and rear stalls. *(Courtesy of* The Architects' Journal, *ph: Wm. J. Toomey.)*

arrangement with a central vomitory.

The 43ft. by 20ft. screen looks huge today and is unmasked at the base where it meets a carpeted platform (the old Curzon's screen was 16ft. by 12ft.). There are no screen curtains: patterns of light play on the screen at intervals.

The Bardot/Moreau western *Viva Maria!* re-opened the Curzon. Programming has tended to favour English-language films as much as

subtitled pictures with *Jean de Florette* and *The Comfort of Strangers* among more recent hits. Quite apart from its choice of films, its brightly illuminated screen, high projection standards, excellent sightlines, exceptionally comfortable seating, and early introduction of a 'no smoking' policy have made it one of the West End's most relaxing cinemas, marred only by the absence of screen tabs.

2 February 1967
Odeon Marble Arch
Edgware Road, Marble Arch

The new cinema was a lavish replacement for the old Odeon, designed by T. P. Bennett & Son as part of a £2m. scheme that included an office block behind. The auditorium sits on the corner above shops at street level with the cinema entrance displaced to Edgware Road where stairs and an escalator take patrons up to their seats. The Odeon seated 1,360 and includes a circle. The projection box is at the rear of the stalls. The screen was the largest in the country, 75ft. by 30ft. at maximum, with a depth of curvature of 17ft. The auditorium is attractively spacious with curtained side walls that are partially obscured by rough-surfaced panelling. The vertical ribs echo those externally.

The cinema opened with *A Funny Thing Happened on the Way to the Forum*. It has had difficulty securing films with real commercial potential for premiere runs and has often taken over big hits after they've been broken in at the Odeon Leicester Square. When the Odeon Marble Arch had a 70mm film like *Die Hard* to occupy the whole of its vast screen, the effect was truly spectacular from the centre of the stalls, akin to being engulfed by Cinerama in the Fifties and Sixties.

With this enormous screen, the Odeon was the logical choice of venue for the restored 70mm version of *Lawrence of Arabia*. But special showings of the film revealed that the deep curve of the screen distorted the emphasis on the flat desert horizon and director David Lean

☐ Left, side wall treatment of the CURZON *(courtesy of* The Architects' Journal, *ph: Wm. J. Toomey).* Above, CURZON in March 1991, showing entrance (between the display cases) on Hertford Street *(ph: Allen Eyles).*

☐ Front stalls and screen for 70mm presentation at ODEON MARBLE ARCH in 1984 *(ph: Allen Eyles).*

□ **ODEON MARBLE ARCH in 1984 with its former deep curved screen for showing 70mm prints** *(ph: Allen Eyles).*

protested. As a result, a new flatter screen was installed (the old screen was cut down to be installed at the State Grays). Although the new screen is reportedly larger than the old one, the effect is not the same. One is too aware of the surrounding masking, whereas the old screen seemed to continue the line of the side walls. . . Huge it may be, but the new screen is nowhere near as enveloping.

Even so, the Odeon deserves to be supported for providing the big screen experience. Alas, an underexploited attempt to promote its huge screen by a season of 70mm prints in July 1990 merely demonstrated that the best films shot in that process are no longer available, while the boast that the films which were found were being presented "on the largest screen in the United Kingdom" seemed to have been confined to the sign above the entrance.

□ **Left, exterior of the ODEON MARBLE ARCH in 1984 and, right, entrance on Edgware Road in March 1991** *(both ph: Allen Eyles).*

12 October 1967
Odeon St. Martin's Lane
The Lane
Lumiere
42/9 St. Martin's Lane

This 737-seat underground cinema (architects: Casson, Condor & Partners) was a completely new addition to the West End within a new office block deep in theatreland (although the nearby Coliseum was on films at the time the Odeon opened). The seating is on one stepped floor and there was originally a suspended screen (44ft. by 20ft.). This had no curtains and there was wrap-around side masking that was used when 'scope proportions weren't needed. The side walls and ceiling were plain, with carpeting forming a dado up to door height.

The Odeon got off to a successful start with a reserved seat run of *Thoroughly Modern Millie* lasting until 14 August 1968. It then opened mostly dodgy films for short runs until *Anne of the Thousand Days* transferred in on 22 April 1970 and ran until 3 June 1971. It seemed to need a major attraction to draw cinemagoers up St. Martin's Lane and there weren't enough to go around the Rank West End houses. At some point conventional curtains were put up in front of the screen.

From 20 July 1975 the Odeon became a permanent home for old and new Walt Disney pictures. Doormen disguised as cartoon figures welcomed patrons and the interior was dressed up with Disney motifs. This policy continued for almost five years before the Odeon was returned to conventional programming on 10 July 1980. It quickly became a white elephant but showed what it could do if only it were given the right film when *Being There* did capacity business for weeks on end with ticket touts on the pavement at evening performances.

Rank made a feeble attempt to turn it into a semi-art house from 5 November

☐ The LUMIERE in March 1991 *(ph: Allen Eyles).*

1981, calling it the Lane (or The Lane in St. Martin's Lane, obviously inspired by the success of the Screen on the Green at Islington). Rank didn't have the know-how to make a success of it and following a disastrous repertory season of British classics it closed on 2 October 1982 to be taken over by Artificial Eye, the specialised distributor which already operated Rank's former Camden Plaza and wanted its own more central outlet. The company spent £40,000 over the next few days, including a new lighting scheme to highlight the shape of the rather plain basement auditorium, the addition of Dolby stereo and the introduction of screen curtains. The cinema re-opened as the Lumiere on 7 October with advertising that sought to link it to the trendy, cinema-less Covent Garden scene. The opening attraction was *Hammett* which astonished the film trade with its huge success here. Though it tailed off more

than expected later on during its 13-week run, *Hammett* breathed new life into the building, which has since caught on firmly to become one of the most successful art houses with a combination of Artificial Eye's own releases and those of other companies.

☐ As the ODEON ST. MARTIN'S LANE in 1967 (note absence of screen tabs and "floating" screen) *(courtesy of* The Architects' Journal).

12 January 1969
Cinecenta 1·2·3·4
Cannon Panton Street
Panton Street

"Four shots to start a cinema revolution!" promised the ingenious campaign that launched the Cinecenta, Europe's first four-in-one cinema. Cinecenta was created out of the old Compton group of companies by their new owner, Leslie Elliot, as a distribution and exhibition company to bring to audiences a whole range of artistic and provocative films of minority appeal. Besides the Panton Street complex, the company had embarked on new cinemas at Bradford and Sheffield and bought up and begun to totally modernise the Globe at Putney. An American design consultant, Harry Gordon, was engaged to create a distinctive image for the cinemas to completely differentiate them from anybody else's.

The space in Panton Street had originally been earmarked for car parking but this was now restricted to the area behind. Nigel Farrington of Cassidy, Farrington & Dennys was the architect for the cinema complex. There were four auditoria seating 138, 154, 150 and 145 and served by mirror periscope projection. On the Sunday night of opening, an offbeat new British film *Wonderwall* was presented on all screens. On the following day, it played on one screen only with three new Cinecenta releases starting their runs: two quality choices, *Les Biches* and the Swedish *Who Saw Him Die?*, plus the sexploitative *The Sinning Urge*.

The cinemas were rather cramped and claustrophobic and failed to start a cinema revolution. But they have stayed in business, coming under the management of the Star circuit (when it took over Cinecenta's circuit in December 1979) and then under Cannon (which took over Star on 30 August 1985 and renamed the cinemas Cannon on the following 6 December). Under Cannon, the four screens have normally been used to continue runs of films that have proved popular in bigger West End cinemas. The complex was refurbished in 1989, the exterior being repainted in two broad vertical bands, a brash red at entrance level and a dark blue higher up.

21 December 1970
ABC 1 & 2
Cannon Shaftesbury Avenue
135 Shaftesbury Avenue

The 1931 Saville Theatre seems to have escaped any cinema use (except, marginally, for the film combined with live action in the Czech *Magic Lantern* show in 1961) but it would have adapted well, being modern in design (architects: T.P. Bennett & Son). When EMI, the new owners of the ABC circuit, were persuaded that it should have a West End flagship (the Regal Marble Arch had been the last one, up to 1940), the Saville Theatre was available. Even with only 1,200 seats, it was too large by 1970 for straightforward adaptation.

Under a scheme drawn up by William Ryder & Associates, the interior was

☐ **ABC SHAFTESBURY AVENUE in January 1984** *(ph: Keith Skone).*

☐ **CINECENTA in 1969: exterior** *(from BFI Stills, Posters and Designs collection)* **and one of the auditoria** *(courtesy of* **The Architects' Journal***).*

□ Part of the front elevation of the CANNON SHAFTESBURY AVENUE in 1991 showing some of the freize depicting "Drama Through the Ages" (ph: Allen Eyles).

ripped out to make way for a 616-seat ABC 1 above a 581-seat ABC 2 at a cost of £600,000, creating two very comfortable, spacious but undistinguished cinemas. The striking exterior with its plaques of "Art Through the Ages" and its 130ft. bas-relief freize depicting "Drama Through the Ages" (by Gilbert Bayes) was fortunately little affected. A large rotating sign capped by an illuminated red globe was erected to draw attention to the cinema, especially from busy Cambridge Circus.

At the time, EMI had its own production programme that was expected to fuel the new twin, but this was soon curtailed. One of its productions, *The Railway Children*, opened ABC 2, with *There's a Girl in My Soup* on ABC 1. The cinemas have not been a spectacular success, largely because they are a little bit out of the way. Following Cannon's takeover of the ABC circuit from EMI, they were given the Cannon name from Friday 17 October 1986. With large screens, excellent sightlines and general spaciousness, they are among the West End's best auditoria. They have continued to function on a varied diet of concurrent first runs, exclusive lesser first-runs, and moveovers from other West End venues.

19 January 1972
The Bloomsbury Cinema
ABC Bloomsbury
EMI International Film Theatre
Gate Two
Gate Bloomsbury 1 & 2
Renoir
Brunswick Square, Bloomsbury

This was a 490-seat underground cinema included at a cost of £300,000 in the Brunswick Square development of 660 flats, 88 shops, two pubs, two restaurants, a supermarket and two subterranean floors of parking space for 800 cars. It was the first British venture of the American Walter Reade Organisation. Although it was a mile away from Leicester Square, president Walter Reade felt that it had a huge potential audience of young people, college students and nurses, within walking distance of the cinema.

The Bloomsbury Cinema opened as an art house with Michael Cacoyannis's *The Trojan Women*. Structural pillars towards the rear limited seating on the single sloping floor, creating V-shaped swathes of open space behind them. Seats were a new type of pedestal chair with blue stretch nylon covers. Innovatory features of the cinema's operation were free coffee, reduced afternoon prices, and higher prices at week-ends.

Through a combination of poor films, an uninviting exterior (a small glass box in an arid concrete setting) and too high prices (did Reade know how cheap and plentiful were the 16mm shows at the various universities around?) the cinema provided its American owners with a headache. Five other cinemas planned for the Greater London area never materialised and it was administratively

□ Two shots of the auditorium of THE BLOOMSBURY CINEMA in 1972.

difficult to run just one cinema so far from home.

EMI took over the cinema on 4 May 1974, renaming it the ABC, then changing it to the EMI International Film Theatre from 27 January 1977 with a policy of offbeat foreign and independent films. A little over a year later, on 15 February 1978, EMI thankfully rented the property to Barbara and David Stone's Cinegate company, which was operating the Gate at Notting Hill. It re-opened as the Gate

□ As the EMI INTERNATIONAL FILM THEATRE (but still retaining BLOOMSBURY sign) in 1977 (ph: Keith Skone).

□ Left, as the RENOIR in March 1991 (ph: Allen Eyles). Above, bar area with "cracked ice" carpeting as modernised in 1986 (courtesy of Artificial Eye).

28 September 1972
Oscar 1
Focus 1
The Soho Cinema
6/10 Brewer Street

The first Brent Walker cinema venture (it was then the G. & W. Walker Group) was the conversion of the ground floor of Isow's restaurant, already owned by the company, into a 184-seat cinema to plans drawn up by Dennis Birch. It was called Oscar 1 because the Walkers had already begun work on two further cinemas across the road. The opening attraction was the Hollywood comedy *What's Up Doc?*, following its London general release. Audiences proved to be predominantly local.

Following pressure from the Academy of Motion Picture Arts and Sciences, who award the annual Oscars, the cinema's name was changed to Focus 1 from 11

Two on 23 February 1978 with Derek Jarman's *Jubilee* and was later converted into twin cinemas, becoming the Gate Bloomsbury 1 & 2, each seating 266, from 24 September 1981. The division down the centre of the original cinema was awkward, leaving exceptionally lofty and angular auditoria, with the screens set high up.

Cinegate closed the building for an 'indefinite period' after showings of *The Outcasts* in 1 and *The Shooting Party* in 2 on Wednesday 30 October 1985, just a few days before shutting down the Gate at Notting Hill. EMI declared that they were given no advance warning of the Bloomsbury closure. Reclaiming the site, EMI leased it to another art film distributor and exhibitor, Artificial Eye, who redecorated and re-opened the two screens as the Renoir Russell Square from Friday 9 May 1986 with *Vagabonde* in 1 and *No Surrender* in 2. By continuing runs of films opened at Artificial Eye's other venues, and opening the occasional difficult foreign film as a first run, Artificial Eye seem to have succeeded in turning this location into a viable one for cinema use.

□ THE SOHO CINEMA. Below, auditorium in 1972 *(from BFI Stills, Posters and Designs collection)*. Above right, exterior circa 1977 *(ph: Keith Skone)*.

April 1974. By this time it had settled down to showing sex and kung fu films. It closed on 1 February 1976 to be taken over by a new management and re-named the Soho Cinema from 4 March 1976, showing sex films (from 1980, on a club basis) and contributing to the area's sleazy image. It was closed in 1983 after new licensing regulations were introduced for 'adult' cinema clubs.

Today it is the home of Madame Jo-Jo's nightclub.

12 May 1973
Minema
45 Knightsbridge

The Savoy Hotel group opened this 68-seat cinema adjacent to their new Berkeley Hotel. Unlike the cinema in the May Fair Hotel, this one has direct access from the street. It has been operated by The Minema Ltd., an independent company wholly owned by Savoy, and it has confounded sceptics by surviving and carving out a very distinctive niche for itself, premiering some films (it opened with the Czechoslovakian *Sweet Games of Last Summer* plus *The Arp Statue*) and shrewdly selecting recent specialised pictures that have stacked up lengthy runs here. (*The Draughtsman's Contract* lasted six months and *My Brilliant Career* also held for several months.) Evidently its comfortable, air-conditioned viewing conditions and its isolated position, combined with its smart booking policy, have done the trick. Its continuing success prompted Rank to open five cinemas of similarly minimal size next to the Odeon Leicester Square in 1990.

□ **THE MINEMA. Exterior view in March 1991** *(ph: Allen Eyles)*. **Auditorium in 1973** *(from BFI Stills, Posters and Designs collection).*

14 June 1973
Scene 1·2·3·4
Premiere 1-2-3 and
Cinémathèque
Swiss Centre, Wardour Street

This was a £300,000 scheme that added four cinemas three floors up to the already functioning Swiss Centre, reached by lift or stairs from an entrance in Wardour Street.

Scene 1 is at the rear with 110 seats and its own projection suite which uses a periscope system. Scenes 2, 3 and 4 — seating 113, 116 and 137 — have a combined projection suite with direct projection in 2 and 4 and a lateral periscope mirror system for 3. They spread across the third floor space with Scene 4 occupying a rotunda feature at the Leicester Square corner of the Swiss Centre, seating audiences in a circular auditorium.

Pasolini's *The Canterbury Tales* opened the complex on all four screens, using only two prints as it was possible to run a single print through the projectors for Scenes 2, 3 and 4. At the time it was reported that the Star group had leased the cinemas for less than £25,000 per year, excluding rates. Star programmed the four Scenes with current hits. Control passed to Cannon from 30 August 1985, and the four screens were refurbished and renamed the Premiere from Friday 22 November with a new policy of showing specialised films. Opening attractions under this policy were *Colonel Redl* in 1, *When Father Was Away on Business* in 2, *The Boys Next Door* (world premiere) in 3, and in the fourth screen called the Cinémathèque a revival of *Citizen Kane*. Although the policy of showing old films in the Cinémathèque was soon dropped, its name has been retained, although it is also referred to as Screen 4 in advertising.

The four screens have increasingly specialised in subtitled foreign films, many of them Cannon's own releases (until its withdrawal from this area), and high standards of selection have been maintained. Unfortunately, the awkward access from the street, the cramped auditoria and indirect projection are bad drawbacks, but they have proved no deterrent to patrons determined to see films not usually showing elsewhere in London.

☐ **SCENE 1·2·3·4 at the Swiss Centre in 1984** *(ph: Keith Skone).*

21 June 1973
Oscar 2 & 3
Focus 2 & 3
Astral 1 & 2
5/7 Brewer Street

These two luxurious mini-cinemas, seating 142 and 156 seats, were created out of former shops at a cost of over £150,000 (architect: Dennis Birch), and both opened with a charity premiere of *Save the Tiger* with star Jack Lemmon in attendance and cutting the tape. Projection was from two machines with "cakestands" in the basement, one of them projecting directly into Oscar 3, the other using periscope-style mirrors to send a picture up to ground floor Oscar 2.

The cinemas were re-named Focus 2 and 3 on 11 April 1974. After groping around for product (even a Humphrey Bogart season of classics was tried), owners G. & W. Walker Group leased them to Craway Securities from 1 July 1974. They were renamed Astral 1 and 2 and continued the sex film programming that had become prevalent at the twin screens. Following a fire, they were closed for many months in 1976. They closed again in late January 1980.

In 1984, the entrance area had become an amusement arcade with video games but by April 1987 the cinemas were operating again as the Astral 1 & 2. With the demise of the Moulin complex in April 1990, they began advertising more prominently as one of London's last remaining 'adult' cinemas, although there were now separate entrances and payboxes for each screen, the original one in the centre of the block and one on the corner with Rupert Street.

☐ **ASTRAL 1 & 2 circa 1977 with entrance behind lamp post** *(ph: Keith Skone).*

22 December 1977
Classic 1·2·3·4·5 Oxford Street
Cannon
Oxford Street

Built below ground level in the building that was formerly the Lyons Corner House at the Tottenham Court Road end of Oxford Street, this was originally a four-screen complex. It opened with *Sinbad and the Eye of the Tiger* in 323-seat Classic 1, *The Hiding Place* (which proved a big success) in 234-seat Classic 2, *Death Is Child's Play* in 184-seat Classic 3, and *Wizards* in 228-seat Classic 4. A licensed bar was added early in 1978. Classic 5 opened on 23 August 1979 with only 76 seats, originally showing 16mm prints. The complex generally shares in multiple screen openings of big new films.

☐ **CANNON OXFORD STREET in March 1991** *(ph: Allen Eyles).*

2 March 1978
Sherlock Holmes Centa 1 & 2
The Screen on Baker Street
96/98 Baker Street

These twin underground cinemas, seating 123 and 117, were the parsimonious replacement for the memorable Classic when the site was redeveloped to provide four floors of shops and office space, leaving only the narrowest of entrances for reaching the two screens below. The still expanding Cinecenta chain opened them with the imaginative (if a little misplaced) Sherlock Holmes name and the Star group took over Cinecenta in December 1979. Like the nearby, larger Times Centa twins under the same management, the Sherlock Holmes twins generally played mainstream attractions but their smaller capacities made them difficult to operate and Star gave up after the last performance on Wednesday 7 September 1983 of *Gandhi* in 1 and *Tootsie* in 2.

Independent exhibitor Romaine Hart (The Screen on the Green, The Screen on the Hill) leased the complex, commenting "It failed because of unimaginative programming, non-existent promotion, and a genuinely unattractive cinema. We can improve the place in all three respects." The cinemas were gutted and completely re-designed with a striking pink and grey colour scheme: grey ceilings, grey drapes on the walls, grey carpet with a pattern of pink dots, and pink seats imported from Paris. The screens are uncurtained and a no smoking policy has been established. Re-named The Screen on Baker Street, the cinemas re-opened on Friday 3 February 1984 with the 95-seat no. 1 screen participating in the premiere run of *Lianna* and the 100-seat no.2 screen taking over the revival of *Rear Window* from the Screen on the Hill, Hampstead.

Within a confined space, the best has been done to create an inviting atmosphere, including a bar area offering coffee and health drinks. The site has comfortably established itself with a flexible policy, mainly of follow-up runs of the more sophisticated West End hits.

☐ **THE SCREEN ON BAKER STREET in 1984** *(ph: Allen Eyles).*

14 August 1980
Gate Mayfair
May Fair Hotel, Stratton Street

Since the early Sixties, the luxurious 55-seat cinema in the hotel basement had functioned as the Starlight Club, a haven for cinema buffs with screenings (changed daily) of old movies on 16mm and 35mm. As attendances declined, the hotel's owners decided to withdraw their subsidy and turn it into a conference room. However, David and Barbara Stone of Cinegate stepped in to make it the Gate Mayfair for extended runs of new films, mostly foreign, beginning with the West German *The Consequence*. Films tended to transfer here from the other Gates at Notting Hill and Bloomsbury (Russell Square). Seating came down to only 48, making it even more minimal in size than the Minema, and it closed on 30 April 1984 with *The Leopard*.

□ **THE SCREEN ON BAKER STREET in 1984. Screen One at top, Screen Two below.** *(Both ph: Allen Eyles.)*

30 July 1981
Classic 1·2·3 Tottenham Court Road
Cannon Tottenham Court Road
Central Cross, 30 Tottenham Court Road

Three underground cinemas were included at the northern end of the huge Central Cross redevelopment, occupying the site of the former Carlton/Berkeley and Majestic/La Continentale. The cinemas were leased for twenty-five years by Classic. They have the advantage of an eye-catching neon display on an adjacent side wall of older property which juts out across the pavement.

The complex has a generous amount of space with a large foyer area and a high-ceilinged main auditorium — Classic 1 with 328 seats — that has a traditional proscenium arch, screen curtains (with pelmet), and a vestigial orchestra pit housing footlights. The side walls are curtained over but globe light fittings illuminate the stereophonic speakers positioned above them in a successful attempt to provide some decorative interest. With its large screen, Classic 1 is a very acceptable addition to the West End line-up. Classic 2 (145 seats) and 3 (137 seats) are long and narrow with lower ceilings but the floors are stepped providing a clearer view of the screen than in most minis and the globe light fittings reappear. Opening presentations were *Condorman* in 1, *S.O.B.* in 2 and *The Great Muppet Caper* in 3. A licensed bar serves all three screens. Programming tended to be more specialised than at the close-by Oxford Street Classic, and foreign films often featured in the choice on offer. Following Cannon's tie up with foreign film distributor Gala, Screen 3 was even re-named the Berkeley from Friday 16 November 1984 and dedicated to specialised films, beginnning with a Truffaut season, but this was dropped after a few months. As with other Classics, the site became known as the Cannon from Friday 6 December 1985. Foreign films had largely disappeared by the end of the Eighties in favour of premiere runs of more specialised American films (*Sex, Lies and Videotape* was a huge hit here) and moveovers of big Hollywood productions.

□ **CLASSIC TOTTENHAM COURT ROAD in 1984. Exterior** *(ph: Keith Skone)* **and two of the cinemas** *(ph: Allen Eyles)* **– largest one and (below) one of the two smaller auditoria with reefer curtains to allow a bigger screen.**

Metro

Rupert Street

In May 1983, The Other Cinema, specialist distributors of avant garde and political films, applied to the GLC Arts and Recreation Committee for funding to create a central London venue for independent and 'progressive' film and video. (The Other Cinema's earlier attempt to establish such an outlet in 1976/7 at the Scala, Tottenham Street, is recorded elsewhere.) An empty basement shell, originally designated for fringe theatre use, was available within the Trocadero Centre at Piccadilly Circus. A grant of £270,000 from the Arts and Recreation Committee covered most of the construction and equipment costs. A grant for video projection equipment was provided by Channel 4 Television. The total cost of the scheme was put at £345,000.

Though a rather incongruous addition to the Trocadero Centre's mass-appeal entertainment attractions (the Guinness World of Records and the London Experience), the Metro was disassociated from it by having a completely separate entrance on a side street amid exits and delivery entrances for the main complex. Above a stylish canopy is a flat, plain wall which was originally intended to be decorated with a huge projector pointing out to the street and with moving searchlights (mounted on the canopy) playing over the surface.

The two auditoria are below ground, Metro 1 seating 196 in what was always designated as auditorium space, and Metro 2 seating 100 in what was to have been the back stage area when live theatre use was planned. The auditoria are reached through a corridor exhibition space, and there is also a bar. The design was by Burrell Foley Associates and is an odd mixture of bare concrete, exposed ventilation ducts, and attractive art deco features of curving walls, metalwork staircases and signs. (No doubt the

☐ Exterior of the CLASSIC TOTTENHAM COURT ROAD in 1984 *(left, ph: Keith Skone; above, ph: Allen Eyles).*

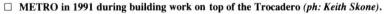

☐ **METRO in 1991 during building work on top of the Trocadero** *(ph: Keith Skone).*

overall starkness reflects financial limitations, but it seems appropriate to the serious nature of the programming policy.) The two cinemas themselves seem rather claustrophobic (especially the smaller) but they do have the considerable advantages of well-stepped rows of comfortable seating giving clear sightlines and very large screens for the size of auditoria (though without curtains).

Operated by Metro Pictures, a specially-formed offshoot of The Other Cinema, the cinemas opened with Jean-Luc Godard's controversial *Hail Mary* in 1 and a Chinese American comedy *Dim Sum* in 2. Chinese films for the Soho Chinese community have been shown on Sundays and weekday afternoons. Though required to be commercially self-sufficient, the cinemas have in general fulfilled their original purpose by concentrating on highly specialised films that would not get shown anywhere else in the West End (except for the ICA). The Metro has certainly established its own, more esoteric image distinguishing it from the Curzons and Cannon's Premiere art house.

☐ **Inside the METRO in 1985, with view of largest auditorium.** *(Courtesy of The Other Cinema.)*

20 March 1987
Curzon Phoenix
Phoenix Street

In March 1986, construction began on this 212-seat cinema which was built onto the Phoenix Theatre, using former parking space. Originally estimated at £545,000, it was reported to have cost over £700,000. Tickets to the cinema are sold from one of the windows in the entrance to the Phoenix Theatre and the auditorium is reached through the magnificent 1930 foyer of the theatre. After this, the cinema's plain decor is an anticlimax – but it was still a remarkable undertaking, having only one screen and being built for its own sake at ground level without the benefit of offices or flats to provide any other income.

The auditorium is box-shaped with its parallel side walls carpeted in dark blue strips laid in horizontal bands. The most original feature is the flat ceiling which consists of rows of slats extending across the auditorium that open like a Venetian blind when a film is being shown to let sound pass from speakers installed in the space above and that are closed when the house lights are on at intervals to form a reflective metallic surface.

The Curzon Phoenix opened with the premiere run of a Russian film, *Come and See*. It has occasionally premiered other new releases of limited appeal but more often takes features over from the larger Curzon Mayfair and Curzon West End, which was the intention when it was built.

Though the seating seems a little cramped, it is nice to be able to watch a film in such a large space (for the number of seats) with a big screen and bright image.

☐ **The CURZON PHOENIX in March 1991 with its entrance through the Phoenix Theatre** *(ph: Allen Eyles).*

□ **CURZON PHOENIX. Exterior in March 1991** *(ph: Allen Eyles)* **and auditorium in 1987.**

19 April 1990
Odeon Mezzanine
Leicester Square

Until 1989, there was a wide, open passageway along one side of the Odeon Leicester Square, running between the Square and Charing Cross Road. It was used by Odeon patrons emerging from exits on the righthand side of the auditorium and by pedestrians generally as a short cut. Dressing rooms had been built over it near the Charing Cross Road end.

Inspired by the continued success of the Knightsbridge Minema despite its low seating, Rank decided to fit five mini-cinemas into this space. These were built at a cost of £1.5 million to the design of Glyn Miller of Northern Building Design Associates, Poynton, Cheshire.

In their decor and ambience, the cinemas are little different from mini-cinemas anywhere else that have been crammed into a tight space. They have their own ground-floor entrance on Leicester Square, and Odeon 1 seating 60 is on the same level. Up some stairs are located Odeons 2 and 3 – the latter is at the rear, seating 60, while to the front Odeon 2 seats 50 with double-headed projection facilities (i.e. two projectors, one to run the image, the other an unmarried soundtrack) so that it can be hired out as a private screening room for viewing films before proper prints are made. Up further stairs to the top of the extension are to be found Odeons 4 and 5, both seating 60 with projectors that can be linked to show the same print. The five auditoria all have Dolby stereo and screens set high above emergency exits, with the same decor of red side wall drapes, flat ceilings and light green seats patterned with horizontal lines. (In the 50-seat auditorium, the emergency

□ **The ODEON MEZZANINE and the five-screen complex's big brother, the Odeon Leicester Square, in March 1991** *(ph: Allen Eyles)*. **The Angus Steak House nearest camera was the site of an early cinema (see page 17).**

□ **ODEON MEZZANINE entrance in March
1991** *(ph: Allen Eyles).*

exit is in the centre under the screen – in
the others, it is to one side.)

The Odeon Mezzanine opened with
previews for invited audiences through a
tie-up with LBC Radio on 19 April. The
following day, Friday 20 April, it opened
to the public with five films already running in the West End – *The War of the
Roses* (transferring from the huge Odeon
next door), *Look Who's Talking*, *The
Fabulous Baker Boys* (with matinees of
All Dogs Go to Heaven) and *When
Harry Met Sally...*, plus one exclusive
first-run, *Troop Beverly Hills*, which
lasted only a week (while the other
attractions continued). Soon afterwards,
it opened *Leviathan* jointly with the
Odeon Marble Arch. Admission price to
all seats was £6, and the Odeon Mezzanine has proved very popular in its first
few months of operation.

Some Club Cinemas

We are providing notes on serious film clubs and two of the sex cinema clubs that went briefly public.

BIJOU/ESSENTIAL/ROXIE, 76 Wardour Street: a former preview theatre had become the Bijou Cine Club for uncensored sex films when Derek Hill, who had run the New Cinema Club hiring various screens since the Sixties, took it over as his own permanent base, in his words turning a Wardour Street tarthouse into an art house, renaming it the Essential and screening independent films and revivals from 15 July 1976 to club members at the 118-seat theatre; it became the Roxie under new management in October 1981, showed gay films for a while, but by 1984 had reverted to the kind of programming it had as the Essential. However, the Roxie closed after showing a double-bill of *Come Back to the Five and Dime, Jimmy Dean, Jimmy Dean* and *Trouble in Mind* on Wednesday 25 March 1987. In March 1991, its premises were unoccupied after having been used by the Roxie Cinema Shop with a fine neon display – but selling items unrelated to cinema.

ELECTRIC CINEMA CLUB / COVENT GARDEN CINEMA CLUB, 29 King Street: this 75-seat cinema was created from Strand Electric's Demonstration Theatre and opened on 3 March 1977 with the long-shelved John Huston film *A Walk with Love and Death*, and followed with imaginative retrospectives, planning later enlargement and a bookshop and wine bar; it was linked to the Electric Cinema Club, Portobello Road, and both were programmed by Peter Howden, but it quickly ran into problems, coming under new management and being re-named the Covent Garden Cinema Club in June 1977 and closing suddenly around April 1978.

GLOBAL VILLAGE, Hungerford Arches off Villiers Street: this opened May 1973 with a cinema, two discotheques and a restaurant, for members only, offering an evening's entertainment for £1.50 inclusive. A film club was run during the day as the Arches Film Society before full conversion. *Tales of Mystery* opened here; the public were later admitted to the cinema; films were abandoned by 1975.

ICA, Nash House, The Mall: an ICA Film Society was established here in the Sixties, and some public performances were introduced in 1976; the auditorium was re-opened on 7 January 1981 with 208 seats after reconstruction with a Cinematheque following in April 1981 (movable seats, maximum 50); this has become an important outlet for premiering difficult films but also indulges in imaginative exercises like bringing back 3-D films (an exclusive run of Hitchcock's *Dial M for Murder*); membership of the Institute of Contemporary Arts is necessary for admission but can be acquired on a temporary day basis to visit the cinema which is closed Mondays.

THE OTHER CINEMA/SCALA, 25 Tottenham Street: this 330-seat basement cinema on the site of the Scala Theatre opened 15 October 1976 as a home for the Other Cinema, reviving old films and showing politically engaged, independent and avant-garde pictures outside the commercial mainstream (mostly public screenings, some club showing of uncertificated films), but it failed to attract enough support and closed on 15 February 1977, re-opening as the Scala on 1 June 1978, with daily changes of repertory programming on 16mm and 35mm on a club basis (nominal membership charge), catering for civilised tastes, only to be ousted by Channel 4 when that organisation took over the entire building as its headquarters (the Scala re-opened at Kings Cross).

PANAMA CLUB/DILLY CINEMA, 41 Great Windmill Street: this conversion of a former night club/restaurant rated coverage in the *Architects Journal*; it opened circa January 1966 as the Panama Club, was open to the public as the Dilly from Tuesday 11 May 1976 offering *Cat at Night* plus *Jungle Sex* until circa August 1976. Part of the Compton and later Cinecenta group, it was taken over by Cannon, who renamed it the Cannon Dilly in November 1985. It subsequently lost its own identity to be made part of the Moulin complex which was closed on 12 April 1990.

PIGALLE, Coventry Street: a 96-seat sex film club opened circa 1972 that later went public (5 February 1976 onwards?) but rarely advertised in the press, relying on lurid displays around its narrow entrance to draw customers in the busy Piccadilly Circus area; closed 4 October 1978 when the block was redeveloped into the new Trocadero centre (there was another Pigalle — now Cinema XXX—in Macclesfield Street, Soho).

Video Cinema

When Brent Walker converted a former Woolworth's into the Oxford Village shopping centre in Tottenham Court Road, a unit on the first floor was turned into a cartoon cinema using videotape, closing around the end of 1982; early in 1984 its auditorium stood locked and disused while Encyclopedia Britannica used its entrance space as a display area. Since then, the entire shopping centre has been converted into an HMV music megastore.

Theatres as Cinemas

Virtually every West End theatre, opera house and music hall has been involved in showing films at some time. Here we record the instances that have come to our attention. The detailed history of these buildings is the province of theatre historians.

ADELPHI: played *The Kid from Spain* in 1933, and Warner Bros.' *A Midsummer Night's Dream* with separate performances from 15 March 1936.

☐ **ALHAMBRA THEATRE's Charing Cross Road frontage (more spectacular than its Leicester Square side), just before demolition in 1936** *(ph: John Maltby).* **Replaced by offices of Alhambra House.**

ALHAMBRA: films included in variety programmes from 26 March 1896 for many years; *Broken Blossoms* opened here in 1920, *The Old Nest* in September 1921, also *The Cabinet of Dr. Caligari;* Sunday film shows from 6 October 1929; leased by British International Pictures for approximately £1,000 per week as its second West End shop window (after the Regal Marble Arch), seating 1,400, and showed talkies from Christmas 1929 to April 1931, with some shows concurrent with the Regal, big hits including *Atlantic* (premiered at the Regal), continuing to April 1934; variety resumed, then acquired by Odeon and demolished for new Odeon Leicester Square (last use on 8 October 1936 as a theatre setting for scenes in film *Men Are Not Gods*).

CAMBRIDGE: equipped for showing films when opened on 4 September 1930 and extensively used for day and evening trade shows throughout the Thirties and early Forties; art cinema (Fritz Lang's *M, Der Hauptmann von Koepenick,* etc.) for six months in 1932 under management of Elsie Cohen; became a public cinema under Gala control opening *La Religieuse* on 28 September 1967 and closing on Saturday 13 January 1968 after the run of Paramount's *Will Penny.*

COLISEUM: films included in variety shows before World War One (Kinemacolor a permanent attraction in early 1913) and in early days of talkies; Sunday trade shows held here in 1926; briefly a public cinema from 6 March 1933, opening *King Kong* on 17 April; run of the sensational venereal disease drama, *Damaged Lives,* from August 1933; briefly a newsreel theatre from late September 1940; public cinema for MGM while Empire was being rebuilt, from 6 June 1961 to 19 May 1963, presentations including *Two Weeks in Another Town* and reissue of Hitchcock's *Rope;* then it was taken over by Cinerama for the installation of a giant Cinerama screen and reopened as the Coliseum Cinerama Theatre on Monday 15 July 1963 with *The Wonderful World of the Brothers Grimm,* later attractions including *Grand Prix,* closing in early June 1968 after a revival of *Around the World in 80 Days.*

COVENT GARDEN OPERA HOUSE: film season from 19 December 1921 with *The Three Musketeers.*

EMPIRE: see notes in history of new 1928 Empire cinema.

☐ **HIPPODROME in 1936** *(from BFI Stills, Posters and Designs collection).*

HIPPODROME: films in variety shows before World War One with fire-proof box in centre of stalls; extensive trade show use 1929/30 and three week public run of *The Wonderful Lie* from Monday 24 June 1929; *Where Is This Lady?* from 4 December 1932; *The Great Ziegfeld* from 12 October to 29 November 1936 (transfer from His Majesty's Theatre).

HIS MAJESTY'S: used by MGM for runs of special attractions – *The Great Ziegfeld* (1 September to 11 October 1936); *Romeo and Juliet* (13 October to 6 December 1936); *The Great Waltz* (13 December 1938 – 15 January 1939).

HIS MAJESTY'S: opened *Romeo and Juliet* in November 1936 and *The Great Waltz* on 13 December 1938.

HOLBORN EMPIRE: films shown 1906-09 in variety bills and also possibly in Thirties.

NEW: film season 1907/8.

PALACE: films shows in September 1897 and as part of later variety shows; acquired by Sol Levy in May 1920 and opened as cinema in association with Charles B. Cochran with elaborate stage preludes and separate performances in February 1921, huge hit with *The Four Horsemen of the Apocalypse* from 14 August 1922, but live revues returned in 1923; *Simba* in September 1928 (and one week in April 1930); *The Queen's Necklace* for two weeks in April 1930; daytime trade shows in Twenties and Thirties; intermittent use by MGM for premiere runs of special attractions – *Grand Hotel* from September to early December 1932, *Dinner at Eight* (from 6 September 1933, following stage version here earlier in year), *David Copperfield* (from March 1935), *The Good Earth* (24 March to 13 June 1937), *Gone with the Wind* (shared with Empire and Ritz, ran here from 22 April to 9 June 1940); also showed *The Robber Symphony* from May 1936; season of Soviet films from 3 to 30 November 1957.

PALLADIUM: films in variety programmes before World War One; public cinema briefly from 19 March 1928 with supporting stage shows; silent *Ben-Hur* with new musical accompaniment by Carl Davis as Thames Silents presentation in 1987 London Film Festival; clips of film projected using carbon arcs as part of stage show *Singin' in the Rain* in 1989.

PHILHARMONIC HALL: films in 1920 (Sir Ernest Shackleton in person describing his latest expedition), and in September 1921; *The Four Horsemen of the Apocalypse* in November 1923 (after run at Palace), and later in Twenties, including *The Light of Asia* from October 1926 and *Simba* in late October 1928 (another transfer from Palace).

PHOENIX: René Clair's *Le Million* shown from 22 April into June 1931; very extensive use for trade shows in Thirties and early Forties; public cinema briefly from Wednesday 8 February 1939 with low price policy, films including *Christine;* children's matinees in 1976 and 1977; entrance now provides paybox and access to adjacent Curzon Phoenix cinema auditorium.

☐ **PICCADILLY THEATRE as the home of Vitaphone in 1929.**

PICCADILLY; opened in April 1928 but taken over by Warner Bros. to present its Vitaphone talkies as 'The Vitaphone Theatre' from 27 September 1928 with *The Jazz Singer,* followed by such films as *The Terror, The Singing Fool* (shown first at Regal), *The Divine Lady, On Trial* and *Noah's Ark;* followed by United Artists' *Evangeline* in December 1929; reverted to live theatre by April 1930; films combined with vaudeville from 16 June 1930 for a while; considerable use for trade shows in Thirties; public films with live shows from December 1937 briefly; two weeks as public cinema reviving *Oliver!* from 26 March 1972.

POLYTECHNIC: the original building's Marlborough Hall was the site of the first public film show before a paying audience on 20 February 1896 (show ran until March 9 when it went to the Empire); seasons of Alfred West's Army and Navy pictures (films of military life) from 1898 to 16 April 1910 when Polytechnic closed for rebuilding (West's shows were attended by over 1½ million people in all). See main text for history of later Polytechnic.

PRINCE OF WALES: opened *The Great Dictator* on 16 December 1940 (along with Gaumont and Marble Arch Pavilion; ended here on 23 February 1941); MGM's *An American Romance* from September to 5 November 1944; *The Secret Life of Walter Mitty* from October 1948; *Cinderella* in January 1950.

QUEEN'S HALL: this Regent Street building was turned into a cinema by Blue Halls Ltd. for showing *Antony and Cleopatra* from Christmas 1913 to the end of January.

ROYALTY: this 1960 replacement for the Stoll Kingsway quickly became a cinema when MGM transferred *Ben-Hur* from the closing Empire to run on here from Monday 29 May 1961; later premiere run of *Mutiny on the Bounty*; became Royalty Cinerama Theatre (London's third Cinerama house after the Casino and Coliseum) from 27 November 1963; operated by Gala as their flagship theatre from 1966 for a few years.

☐ **SCALA THEATRE circa 1912 (as displayed in an old film programme).**

SCALA: a full-time cinema with Charles Urban's very popular Kinemacolor shows from 11 April 1911 to late 1913 (some programmes lasted two months or more), then leased to J. Leslie Crown; *Birth of a Nation* premiered here in September 1915; films returned 12 October 1921 with *Orphans of the Storm* opening in 1922; film season started 5 August 1929; scene of a Tribute to Humphrey Jennings on 7 January 1951 in aid of his widow and two daughters; Russian films in late Fifties under auspices of the British Soviet Friendship Society.

THEATRE ROYAL DRURY LANE: had premiere run of *Intolerance* from 7 April 1917 at full theatre prices to disgust of film trade who viewed it as "unfair competition".

TIVOLI: films shown with variety before World War One (later demolished for new Tivoli cinema).

Name Index

Main reference only

ABC Bloomsbury *106*
ABC Shaftesbury Avenue *105*
Academy *35*
Adelphi Theatre *118*
Alhambra Theatre *118*
Apollo Victoria *63*
Arena Picture Theatre *17*
Army and Navy Cinema *39*
Astoria *49*
Astral 1 & 2 *109*
Avenue Pavilion *33*
Berkeley (Mayfair) *80*
Berkeley (Tottenham Court Court) *40*
Bijou (Tottenham Court Road) *23*
Bijou Club (Wardour Street) *117*
Biograph Victoria *15*
Bloomsbury Cinema (Theobalds Road) *43*
Bloomsbury (Brunswick Square) *106*
Bloomsbury Super *43*
Cambridge Circus Cinematograph Theatre *29*
Cambridge Theatre *118*
Cameo Charing Cross Road *20*
Cameo Great Windmill Street *24*
Cameo Moulin *24*
Cameo News Theatre *31*
Cameo-Polytechnic *31*
Cameo Royal *20*
Cameo Victoria *79*
Cannon Baker Street *90*
Cannon Charing Cross Road *29*
Cannon Haymarket *51*
Cannon Moulin Complex *24*
Cannon Oxford Street *110*
Cannon Panton Street *105*
Cannon Piccadilly *74*
Cannon Prince Charles *100*
Cannon Royal *20*
Cannon Shaftesbury Avenue *105*
Cannon Tottenham Court Road *112*
Capitol *46*
Carlton Haymarket *51*
Carlton Tottenham Court Road *40*
Casino *94*
Casino Cinerama *94*
Casino de Paris *18*
Centa *74*
Centre News Theatre *24*
Charing Cross Cinema *18*
Charing Cross Electric Theatre *18*
Charing Cross Fonomatograph Theatre *18*
Cinecenta Panton Street *105*
Cinecenta Piccadilly *74*
Cineclub 24 *20*
Cinema de Paris *20*
Cinema House *25*
Cinephone *92*
Circle in the Square *17*
Circlorama *100*
Classic Agar Street *28*
Classic Baker Street *82*
Classic Cartoon Theatre *71*
Classic Charing Cross Road *20*
Classic Haymarket *41*
Classic Moulin *24*
Classic Oxford Street *110*
Classic Piccadilly Circus *100*
Classic Poly *31*
Classic Royal *20*
Classic Shaftesbury Avenue *95*
Classic Tottenham Court Road *112*
Classic Victoria *79*

Coliseum Theatre *118*
Columbia *95*
Compton Cinema Club *97*
Continentale, La *32*
Corner Theatre *27*
Court *31*
Covent Garden Cinema Club *117*
Covent Garden Opera House *118*
Cupid's *17*
Curzon Mayfair *70, 101*
Curzon Phoenix *114*
Curzon West End *95*
Dilly *117*
Dominion *61*
Electric Cinema Club *117*
Electric Palace Oxford Street *14*
Electric Theatre (Victoria) *15*
Embassy (Holborn) *27*
Embassy (Tottenham Court Road) *92*
EMI International Film Theatre *106*
Empire *54, 98*
Empire 1 *98*
Empire 1, 2 and 3 *98*
Empire 2 *86*
Eros *71*
Essential *117*
Filmcenta *29*
Fitzroy Picture Palace *33*
Focus 1 *107*
Focus 2 & 3 *109*
Forum *17*
Gaiety *18*
Gate Bloomsbury *106*
Gate Mayfair *111*
Gate Two *106*
Gaumont Haymarket *80*
Gaumont News Theatre *33*
G.B. Movietonews Theatre *33*
Global Village *117*
Grafton *27*
Grand Casino *27*
Grand Central *23*
Hippodrome Theatre *118*
His Majesty's Theatre *118*
Holborn Cinema *27*
ICA *117*
Jacey Charing Cross Road *29*
Jacey in the Strand *74*
Jacey Leicester Square *78*
Jacey Marble Arch *90*
Jacey Piccadilly *74*
Jacey Trafalgar Square *77*
Jaceyland *90*
Jardin de Paris *19*
La Continentale *32*
Lansdowne News Theatre *80*
Leicester Square Theatre *68*
London News Theatre *92*
London Pavilion *72*
Londoner, The *97*
Lumiere *104*
Madame Tussaud's Cinema *19*
Majestic *32*
Majestic Picturedrome *32*
Marble Arch Pavilion *40*
Marlborough Hall *31*
Metro *113*
Metropole Victoria *59*
Minema *108*
Monseigneur News Theatre Leicester Square *78*
Monseigneur News Theatre Oxford Street (Marble Arch) *90*
Monseigneur News Theatre Piccadilly *74*
Monseigneur News Theatre Strand *74*
Monseigneur News Theatre Trafalgar Square *77*
Moulin Complex *24*

National Bioscope Electric Theatre *28*
New Egyptian Hall *13*
New Gallery *34*
New Victoria *63*
Odeon Haymarket *97*
Odeon Leicester Square *82*
Odeon Marble Arch *57, 103*
Odeon Mezzanine *115*
Odeon St. Martin's Lane *104*
Odeon Tottenham Court Road *75*
Odeon West End *68*
Olympic *68*
Oscar 1 *107*
Oscar 2 & 3 *109*
Other Cinema, The *117*
Oxford Village cartoon cinema *117*
Palace Theatre *118*
Palais de Luxe *20*
Palladium Theatre *118*
Palm Court Cinema *17*
Panama Club *117*
Paramount Lower Regent Street *47*
Paramount Tottenham Court Road *75*
Philharmonic Hall *118*
Phoenix (Oxford Street) *23*
Phoenix Theatre *118*
Piccadilly Circus Cinematograph Theatre *24*
Piccadilly News Theatre *24, 71*
Piccadilly Theatre *118*
Picture House *35*
Pigalle *117*
Plaza *47*
Polytechnic *118*
Premiere 1-2-3 and Cinémathèque Swiss Centre *109*
Premiere Shaftesbury Avenue *95*
Prince Charles *100*
Prince of Wales Theatre *118, 119*
Pyke House Cinematograph Theatre *23*
Pyke's Cambridge Circus Cinematograph Theatre *29*
Queen's Hall *119*
Regal *57*
Regent Poly *31*
Renoir *106*
Rialto *37*
Ritz *86*
Roxie *117*
Royalty Theatre *119*
St. James' Picture Theatre *44*
Scala *117*
Scala Theatre *119*
Scene 1·2·3·4 *109*
Screen on Baker Street, The *110*
Shaftesbury Pavilion *33*
Sherlock Holmes Centa 1 & 2 *110*
Soho Cinema *107*
Sphere News Theatre *18*
Starlight Club *111*
Stoll Picture Theatre *42*
Strand Cinema Theatre *28*
Strand News Cinema *28*
Studio One *25*
Studio 1·2·3·4 *25*
Studio Two *78*
Studio 4 *78*
Super (Charing Cross Road) *29*
Super (Bloomsbury) *43*
Tatler *29*
Theatre de Luxe *14*
Time News Theatre *90*
Times *90*
Times Centa 1 & 2 *90*
Tivoli *44*
Topical News Theatre *90*
Tussaud's Cinema *53*
Universal *47*

Victoria Picture Hall *15*
Victoria Picture Palace *28*
Victoria Station Cartoon Theatre *69*
Victoria Station News Theatre *69*
Victory *43*
Villiers Cinema *17*
Warner *87*
Warner Rendezvous *87*
Warner West End *87*
West End Cinema Theatre *37*
Windmill *20*